HITCHHIK
TO THE PAST

STUART MACPHERSON

Also by Stuart MacPherson

A Passion for Vincent
A Passion for Quotes

HITCHHIKER'S GUIDE TO THE PAST

STUART MACPHERSON

**Craigdhu
Press**

Published in 2023 by Craigdhu Press

Copyright © 2023 Stuart MacPherson

Stuart MacPherson has asserted hisright to be identified as the author of this Work in accordance with the Copyright, Designs and Patents Act 1988

ISBN Paperback: 978-1-9161462-4-2

E-Book: 978-1-9161462-5-9

A CIP catalogue copy of this book can be found in the British Library.

Published with the help of Indie Authors World
www.indieauthorsworld.com

IndieAuthors
World

CONTENTS

Dedicated to Yun Soon, Ann & Mike, Kristian, Paula

In Memory of Mum & Dad, Doreen & Campbell

CHAPTER 1
THE ANCIENT BRITS

A ncient Britain, not surprisingly, was inhabited by people called Ancient Brits. Some of them were very ancient indeed and they built very ancient ruins to prove it.

Julia Caesar, the Roman Emperor (or Empress - see later) was the first foreigner to clap eyes on the Ancient Brits. In his (or her) book Caesar's Garlic Wars, he described them as uncivilised tribes with long hair and very long moustaches who invariably painted themselves blue. Historians now agree that this was probably an early example of colour coding. They were also extremely fierce and rode around in chariots with knives on the wheels at breakneck speed cutting the legs off any passing pedestrian (see later under "Queen Body Sear's Rebellion: Getting Legless"). This started the ongoing Brit tradition of doing things that foreigners from across the Channel found difficult to understand.

Though uncivilised and illegitimate, the Ancient Brits did a lot of building work constructing many ruins which can still be seen today. The most impressive of these was, of course, Stone Hinge on Salisbury plane, which was difficult to build as rocks from North Wales had to be used and brought all the way down to South England, as there were no local rocks on Salisbury plane. Stone Hinge is thought to be a gigantic sundial, or moondial, or a religious temple in which there were human sacrifices on the Hale stone.

The Ancient Brit priests were called Druids who had long white robes and long white beards and were very fierce, according to Julia Caesar, even fiercer than the ordinary lay-brits. All good druids carried big scythes and sickels to cut the heads off anyone kissing under the mistletoe, which was sacred. Hence the old English expression "necking".

The Brits built many other Hinges, not only of stone but of wood and many other building materials. They also made a large man-made hill shaped like a Christmas pudding called Silbeery hill. The purpose of this has never been clear, but some historians now think it may have been a practical joke at the expense of modern archyologists who have spent years digging down through it, across through it, up through it, diagonally down through it, diagonally up through it, across it and underneath it, looking for a legend-ary golden horse which is supposed to be buried in it. And you can't get any more legendary than that horse. In fact the archyologists have found absolutely zilch in that hill, which has to go down as a result for the Brits: Archyologists nil / Ancient Brits 1.

Besides Hinges and dummy hills the Brits built many barrows or tumours in which they buried important people like druids, architects and tribal chiefs. In fact some now believe that the aforementioned Silbeery hill was for the burial of an extremely important man, perhaps an Emperor, and so is nothing more or less than a gigantic tumour.

It is thought that the first foreigner to actually see Britain, albeit from a respectable distance was also, like the Brits, Ancient, except that he was not an Ancient Brit but an Ancient Greek from Grease called Python. Sailing all the way around it, he named it "Ultima Thule" which in Ancient Greek means "Ultimate Hell". Sensibly he did not land because of the atrocious weather, and he had also noticed that the Blue Brits were obviously not yet ready for Multiculturalism. (Hence the term "True Blue".)

The first people to seriously invade Britain were of course the Ancient Romans, who were very cruel and greedy, but nevertheless CIVILISED. Even more importantly they were also MULTICULTURAL. Thus we must diverge briefly to have a look at Ancient Rome.

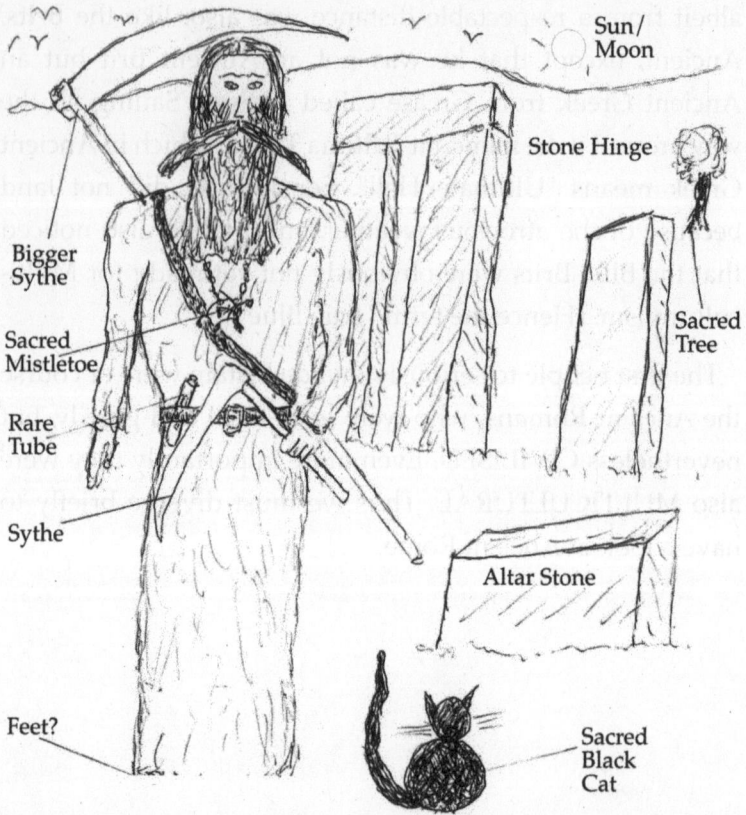

Sun/Moon

Stone Hinge

Bigger Sythe

Sacred Tree

Sacred Mistletoe

Rare Tube

Sythe

Altar Stone

Feet?

Sacred Black Cat

A left-handed Ancient Brit Druid getting his equipment ready to do a bit of sacrificing at this favourite workplace

Also note that back in those days almost everything was sacred including the Sun, the Moon, the stars, Mistletoe, trees, black cats, ravens, geese, springs, wells, rivers & of course the Druids themselves. To kiss under any of these was sacrilege and so, for instance anyone caught kissing under the Moon & Stars by a Druid was said to be Moon-struck, or Starstruck. Even today eerie stories about black cats or ravens are familiar to us all.

ANCIENT ROME

Rome, situated on six hills by the river Tiger in Italy, was built in a day by two legendary twin brothers, Romellus and Remo with the help of the gods[1]. These twin boys had been brought up in childhood and suckled by a she-wolf, and this unusual background was, of course, what made them legendary. If you want to get legendary, there can't be a much better way of doing it than that.

Being legendary, of course, entitled Romellus and Remo to the help of the gods, and so they were able to build Rome in just one day, disproving the famous (but inaccurate) saying. Unfortunately, at this stage, the brothers quarreled over what to call their new city - should it be "Roma" after Romellus or "Rema" after Remo? This controversy was soon resolved by Romellus who threw his brother over the city wall, thus killing him, which is a pretty comprehensive way to settle any argument. Rome became "Roma".

Romellus had one more big problem: all of his new citizens were bachelors & there were no women readily available for marriage. But he noticed that a local tribe called the Sapines (or Saps for short) had plenty of female wives & daughters, and so he hatched a dastardly plot. The Saps were all invited to a giant feast and soon the party hotted up. While the Sapines were revelling & wassailing, the Romans quietly sneaked away and abducted all their wives & daughters back to Rome. Luckily, these women

---

[1] The Romans had the same gods and goddesses as the Ancient Greeks who lived on top of a mountain in Grease called Mt. Olimpus. These included Zeus, Apolo, Diana, Hermes, Miniver, Neptune & Vulcano. But the Romans, unable to pronounce the language which was Greek to them, changed all their names so, for instance, Zeus became Jupiter & Hermes became Mercurial.

thought the whole thing was rather romantic, and so became good Roman wives. The next Roman generation was soon online, so to speak; problem solved Q.E.D.

Before he died, Romellus stamped everything Roman with his famous trademark S.P.Q.R. after his full name: Sydney Poitier Quintin Romellus[2].

The Romans were civilised, but not as civilised as the Greeks of course. Rome started as a Republic, but after Julia Caesar had crossed the famous Ruby Con it became a Republic with Emperors.

The Romans were an earthy lot who liked blood sports in the Coliseum and other entertainment in the circus. They were divided into two classes: The upper class who were called Patricias, or Pansies for short (especially by the working class) and the lower class which were called the Roman Mob or Plebiscites. This was a problem for Emperors as the Mob could often become riotous & even homicidal at times, killing several Emperors as well as many others like Senators. This is why one of the Emperors sagely advised apprentice emperors to "Give them bread and circumstances". Some deluded historians believe that this advice was "Give them cake & circuses", but any scholar worth his salt knows that phrase was never used until much later by Marie-Antoinette (see later under "The French Revolution").

The Romans were outstandingly clean people, and they built and took baths all over the place. So clean were they in

---

[2] In the past confused scholars have taken the view that these initials stand for "The Senate & People of Rome" but any fool knows that the word "of" does NOT start with a "Q"!

fact that they had to build numerous aquaducts to keep up the water supply.

They also built many absolutely straight roads all of which led directly towards, or directly away from Rome - according to which way you happened to be pointing at the time.

But the most important thing about Rome was the Army. However, it is important to note that it was not called an "Army" but Legions. Each Legion had a name and number e.g. The British Legion. The Legions were very well trained & could make many formations, including even one in the shape of a Tortoise which amazed the enemy so much that they often ran away without fighting. These Legions were also experts at construction & could build anything: roads, bridges, walls, castles, toilet blocks, swimming pools, condos & even circuses. With these formidable soldiers, the Romans soon conquered all the known World, except Germany, which was unknown anyway, and Scotland, which was even more unknown. This all became the Roman Empire, of course, but not Holy yet!

ROMAN EMPERORS

Being a Roman Emperor was a risky business as Julia Caesar found out on the Idles of March when he was stabbed on the steps of the Senate by a brute and a lean, hungry man called Cussius. He fell at the feet of a statue of his old enemy, Pompous, shouting, "Oh, you Brute." ("Et ta Brute.")

New Emperors were well-advised to bribe their own palace guards to let them stay alive. Even this was not a surefire winner however, as the palace guard could sometimes get cranky, taking the bribe but then killing the new Emperor anyway. For palace guards new Emperors became a growth industry. Thus life expectancy among Emperors was decidedly short, and if they were not actually killed by their own palace guard, they were still fair game for either (a) the Roman mob (b) the Legions (c) the Senate (d) their wives (a frequent occurence) (e) ambitious relatives or (f) revolting gladiators called Russell Crow. It was tough at the top, and as one Emperor called Trumus once famously said, "The bullet stops here," pointing to his stomach.

Julia Caesar was, of course, the first Emperor of Rome (or Empress). Because of his name, his sexual orientation is a mystery, and some historians think he might have been a she in drag. But Julia was nevertheless a good Emperor/Empress.

Emperor Caesar   OR   *impress Julia?*

THE GREAT CAESAR RIDDLE

There were also some spectacularly bad Emperors. The first of these was de Nero who started off by killing off his mother, brother, wives and in-laws, in fact all his relatives as well as many other individuals, mainly Pansies like Senators, especially if they fell asleep while he was singing, acting or reciting his poetry in the theatre. He scuppered his

Mum by sending her out boating in a special tricks boat, which duly fell apart when she was well out to sea. The fact was that he preferred his catamites and stalagmites to relatives.

Not content with this de Nero then burned the whole of Rome to the ground to claim the insurance money for a new palace. This had the additional advantage of reducing a glut of plebiscites who had been mobbing too much lately. As he watched the flames of burning Rome from a safe distance, de Nero strummed his guitar and sang songs and poetry while roasting chestnuts in the embers. He then blamed the Christians for the fire, and burned them too, as well as sending them into the arena with the lions. (He had to stop this practice however as the gladiators began picketing the Coliseum complaining that Christians & lions were putting them out of a job.) So he continued to burn Christians and soon found that Saints, being full of the Holy spirit, burned particularly well. Because of this, he used the saints to light up the Palace gardens at night.

Even worse than Nero was Caligula, who was mad, bad and exceptionally dangerous to know (with some superlatives). His real name was Emperor Gayus, but he surprisingly preferred his nickname Caligula which in Roman means "Little Boobs". He had already killed another Emperor when he came to the throne: his uncle Tidalwavus whom he suffocated with a pillow. He killed all of his family, including his four sisters, after marrying one of them. He then married his horse and made her a Senator (or Senatress perhaps). Meanwhile anyone became fair game for Little Boobs including Senators (& Senatresses), Patricias, Pansies, Plebs, mobsters and any Roman ladies who took his fancy. He also annoyed the tough Legion N.C.Os while on campaign by giving them passwords like "Give us a kiss", or "See you tonight darling" or even "Who's a pretty boy then?". Finally Caligula decided that he was a God, and not just any god, but the King of the Gods himself, Jupiter. The Romans then decided that he was a suitable case for treatment.

Not surprisingly, Caligula and de Nero met violent ends, but then so did most Emperors whether they were good, bad or just indifferent. Take the first six Emperors for example: Julia - killed by Senators; Augustas - poisoned by his wife; Tidalwavus - suffocated by his nephew; de Nero - killed by soldiers; Caligula - killed by angry N.C.Os; and Claude - poisoned by his wife. Thus the final score was Wives 2, soldiers 1, N.C.Os 1 & nephews 1: a clear victory for the wives.

As can be seen being a Roman Emperor was a dodgy business. It wasn't too healthy being related to an Emperor either, especially if he was Caligula or de Nero.

THE ROMAN INVASION OF BRITAIN

Julia Caesar had already conquered Egypt, Spain & Gaul (as described in his book "Caesar's Garlic Wars") and he felt that to leave Britain out would be untidy. It was also rumoured that the Brits had gold mines. So he set sail with his legions and crossed the Channel. As he neared the beach he caught sight of a reception party of wild, true blue, long-haired, true Brits waiting for him and was not impressed, making the well-known comment "VENI, VIDI, VICI", which meant that they were vain, weird & vicious. But his seasick legions felt differently and did not like the look of the Brits at all as they were evidently very unfriendly, and not in the least multicultural. Moreover, as the ships got closer to the shore these savages, encouraged by even savager druids, began shouting and throwing spears, arrows, rocks, and other less pleasant things. The Romans also noticed that they all wore long red & white scarves and were chanting something which sounded like "'Ere we go, 'Ere we go, 'Ere we go! / 'Ere we go, 'Ere we go, 'Ere we go-oo!" ect. All very uncouth to be sure.

Not surprisingly then the Legions refused to get out of the ships, making the excuse that their feet would get wet (they only wore sandals after all) hence the expression "getting cold feet". So in the end Julia himself (or herself) had to strip off and dive in shouting, "Come in, boys, the water's lovely," before they would wade to the beach.

The Romans used a lot of their hi-tech machines in the war against the Brits like ballistics - for shooting big spears, manglewurzels for throwing even bigger rocks, and siege towers or balfries. All the Brits had against all this hi-tech was their high speed chariots, and though they drove these furiously, they could not cope with all the flying rocks. The Romans had them beat (or at least thought they did).

One day the legions captured one of these Brit chariots and later, after stumps had been drawn at close of battle, one of their officers, a vigorous young man, decided to try the thing out. But when he pressed the self-starter the chariot took off at breakneck speed into the distance in a huge cloud of dust. The soldiers watched amazed as the dust cloud disappeared over the horizon in just a few seconds, never to be seen again. As for the officer, he staggered back into the camp three days later alone, his face white, shaking like a leaf, hatless, shoeless and his uniform in rags minus horses and chariot. Even his luxurious black hair had turned white as snow. And when one of the soldiers asked him what had happened all he could say was: "No brakes, dodgy steering, no brakes, dodgy steering, no brakes, dodgy steering," over and over and over again. The poor man had to be invalided out of the army with "Chariot Fatigue".

ROMAN BRITAIN

Now that peace had been restored the Romans began doing their usual Roman thing, building cities, villas, bridges all over the place, and of course straight roads all leading directly to Rome. They also, as was their wont, built many Roman baths. The biggest of these was at Bath, which already had hot running water laid on. This Bath bath could take a hundred people at a time. They also encouraged the natives to use these baths to wash all the blue paint off, get a decent shave and put on clean Roman togs, thus changing into Romano-Brits instead of plain Brits. Some did, others did not as they didn't like all the Roman inventions, especially not taxes, and this led to trouble.

QUEEN BODY SEAR'S REBELLION: GETTING LEGLESS

One of those against the tax was the feisty Queen Body Sear of the Icky tribe, and she refused to pay. The Romans now made a serious mistake by having her whipped, and her daughters too for good measure, for tax evasion, money-laundering & failing to fill in her tax return correctly. Just how serious this mistake was, they were about to find out!

Body Sear now raised her own tribe, and was soon joined by many other tribes like the Brigantes or brigands & attacked the Legions, riding into the battle herself with long knives fixed to her chariot wheels, chopping off Roman legs with her wheels & Roman heads with her massive sword. This seriously reduced the stature of the Legions, and those soldiers who still had legs found they had also got cold feet and ran away as fast as they could go. (Hence the old expression "Getting legless".)

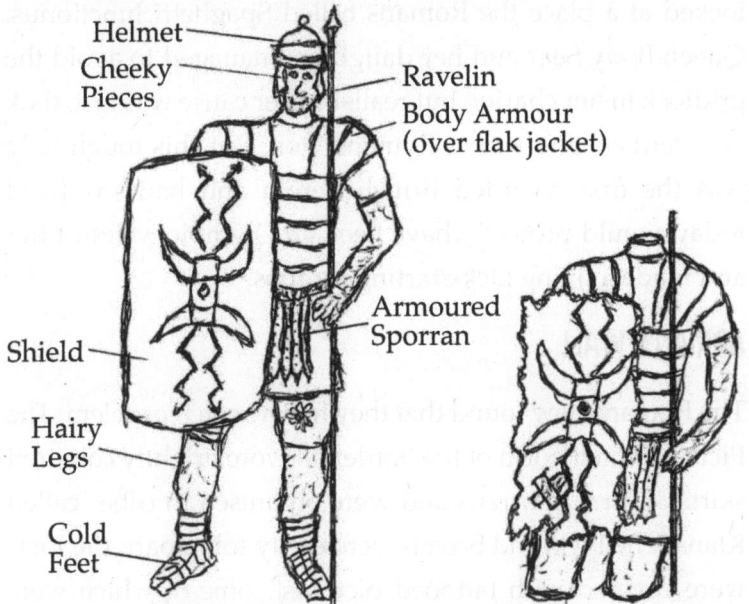

Helmet
Cheeky Pieces
Ravelin
Body Armour (over flak jacket)
Shield
Armoured Sporran
Hairy Legs
Cold Feet

A Roman Legion in full fighting fig. — After a course of the Body Sear treatment

Having thus disposed of the Legions, Body Sear and her hoard of revolting true-blue Brits, plundered & burned every new Roman city they could find, putting everyone to the sword, naturally, including a lot of Roman veterinaries who had retired from the army. The fearsome Queen chopped all the heads & legs off their statues with her sword and chariot wheels, even including the Emperor Claude. This was called accelerated Urban blight. Finally she burned London - not a bad idea at any time. Some people said she got these ideas after reading a book about de Nero (see under "Roman Emperors").

But finally Roman reinforcements arrived. These new legions fought in wedges, which the revolting Brits had not seen before, and so they were defeated at Manchester in spite of help from some friendly local Man. U supporters, and even lost all their carts & wagons which were gridlocked at a place the Romans called Spaghetti Junctionus. Queen Body Sear and her daughters managed to avoid the gridlock in her chariot, but realising her cause was lost, took an overdose and so the Romans won. But this tough lady was the first recorded British heroin and had she lived today, would probably have been an Olympic weight-lifter and made a living kick-starting Jumbos.

ADRIAN'S WALL

The Romans now found that they had a Scotch problem. The Picts & Scotch north of the border all wore brightly coloured skirts & furry sporrans and were organised in tribes called Klans. The Picts and Scotch were easily told apart: the Picts were covered with tattooed pictures, some of which were positive works of art, whereas the Scotch usually made do with a quick paint job. But the Romans soon discovered that they had a good number of antisocial habits which ought to be suppressed. These included drinking an enchanted brown liquid which could not be put near a naked flame by the drum, and then blowing into bags which made hideous noises, and even chucking telephone poles around all over the landscape. Not only that, they talked in an incomprehensible accent, ate stuffed footballs they called Haggis and worshipped a God called Hogmanay.

So the Roman governor Agriculturus decided that in the interest of public order something had to be done about these Highland hooligans, and so marched into Scotland and beat them at Mons Grumpius, as recorded by his son-in-law, the famous Roman historian Taciturnus. But it made no difference, because the Scotch stubbornly refused to become

Romans, or Brits (whom they called Sassafras), or Romano-Brit or indeed anything at all except Scotch, and remorselessly continued to blow in bags & follow their other hideously anti-social customs. Not only that, but the weather up there was so peculiarly awful that the baffled Legions decided to retreat and build a wall along the border instead.

The wall was named after the Emperor Adrian and can still be seen today. It had all mod cons including ensuite forts and guardhouses, swimming pools, tennis courts & real Roman toilets made of stone (which might have been uncomfortable, especially in cold weather). Modern day visitors can still sit on a Roman toilet if they feel that way inclined. The wall was a good thing as it kept the Picts & Scotch in, although they continued to throw telephone poles around, and spitefully make their hideous bag noises at all hours of the day and night just to give the Legions a hard time. Unfortunately all attempts to soundproof the wall failed, and so earplugs became mandatory equipment for all soldiers manning the wall at all times.

Driven out by Wild Pipes and a Horrible Hairy Haggis!

THE END OF THE ROMAN EMPIRE

Eventually the Roman Empire began to be overrun by many different types of barbarians including Vandals, Huns, Goths, Fizzy Goths, Astra Goths, Germans, Franks & Saxons. The worst of these were the Huns under Atitler, but the first to reach Rome and sack it were the Fizzy Goths under their leader Al Eric. Those Fizzy Goths entered Rome easily because some of their number were slaves of the Romans & opened the gates for their pals.

Meanwhile on the orders of the Emperor, the Legions left Britain to the tender mercies of the Picts & Scotch with their horrendous bag wails.

Back in Rome, the barbarian Fizzy Goths did a good, thorough job of sacking & plundering, and then went on a five day binge drinking session - who could blame them after that long hike from Sweden? Unfortunately this was one too many for poor Al Eric who was getting on in years, and he made it to Valhalla. Thus, in spite of severe hangovers, the Fizzy Goths diverted the river Tiger further upstream, and buried their King and all his treasures in the river bed, & after killing any passing Roman who had noticed this, they allowed the river to run back over him. This effectively snookered any local tomb robbers.

After the Fizzy Goths left Rome it was gang-sacked by all the other barbarians in turn: the Huns, Vandals & Astra Goths, among others. Small wonder that the Forum, which can be seen to this day, is still so ruined.

Some years later the Fizzy Goths and Astra Goths became civilised & just plain Goths. They toured all round Europe building gothic cathedrals to make up for the damage they had done in Rome.

As for the Romans, after these repeated harrowing experiences, they all moved to a new, large city called Bigzantium & started a new Empire called the Bigzantine Empire.

THE END OF ROMAN BRITAIN

As the Romans had left, the British had self rule. This might have been a good thing but it wasn't because the Picts & Scotch, all illegal immigrants, swarmed over Adrian's wall plundering, pillaging & looting, without even having the decency to apply for political asylum. The British King, Vortex, now made a fatal mistake by panicking & inviting in another group of illegal immigrants, mercenaries from Germany called Anglos & Saxons, to fight you know who. But the Saxons, under their leaders Hingis & Horser carried long knives and were treacherous. The Scotch continued plundering ect. & the Saxons decided they liked the lifestyle, so they treacherously changed sides. The Anglo-Saxon invasion followed (see later) and all the poor Brits were driven into Whales, where they had to become Welsh.

This concluded the Ancient Brits, and needless to say, the Romans too.

Only one legendary man kept up the fight against the Saxons - the very legendary King Arthur.

Historical Aptitude & Intelligence Test
Test Paper 1: Romans & Brits
(1 hour 30 mins)

Answer between 3 & 13 of the following questions, but on no account more than 13. Answers may be submitted in any language except 4-letter Anglo-Saxon & North Korean. Apologies to N. Korean candidates, but our translator has not been seen since a recent purge by Kim.

N.B. Extra marks will be awarded for the following:-

(a) Correct spelling (b) Pinpoint accuracy (c) A colourful rendition

If candidates have any queries they may ask the invigilator, but they should not expect necessarily to get a sensible answer.

***

1. Was de Nero wrong to burn Rome, Queen Body Sear right to burn London & the Fizzy Goths wrong to sack Rome, or was it the other way round? Be Precise.

2. Discuss the effect on Roman history of the following: (a) Russell Crowe (b) Ben Her (c) Charlton Heston (d) Al Eric (e) Peter Ustinov (f) Caligula's horse. Be dramatic.

3. There is a new historical theory that the Ancient Brits may have built all their hinges, mounds & other ruins to fool modern archyologists. Discuss & evaluate this theory.

4. Was the Greek explorer Python right in naming Britain "Ultima Thule" ("Living Hell")? Discuss this with reference to the following: (i) The weather (ii) Soccer hooliganism (iii) The Sun newspaper (iv) Queen Body Sear of

the Icky (v) Binge drinking (vi) Man. U striker Egon Ronay (vii) New Licensing laws.

5. How did Queen Body Sear reduce the stature of the Legions? Keep it short.

6. Why was the life expectancy of Roman Emperors so much shorter than that of the average Roman? Do not be too graphic.

7. Is there any substance to the theory that Julia Caesar was either: (a) a man (b) a woman (c) a man in drag (d) a woman in drag (e) a transvestite hermaphrodite (f) a clone or (g) none of the above? Keep it clean!

8. Why did the Goths build so many cathedrals? Was this A GOOD THING?

9. Define precisely the origins of the following English expressions: (i) Getting cold feet (ii) Getting Legless (iii) Give them cakes and cir-cumstances (iv) Who's a Pretty boy, then?

10. Why was Adrian's Wall such a good invention. Should it be restored completely?

11. Why were the following against the Geneva Convention: (a) Brit chariots (b) Emperor Caligula (c) Mangel-wurzels (d) Fizzy Goths & (e) Scotch pipes?

12. Were the Romans really so civilised anyway, or was it just a ploy to raise more stealth taxes?

13. Was Britain under the Romans either a Nanny state or a Granny state? If neither, then what the hell was it? Answers should not contain any swearing, 4-letter words or blasphemy whatsoever!

THE END!

H.A.I.T. Test Paper 1:
Model Answer Specimen

At popular request the H.A.I.T. Examining board has agreed to publish several Model specimen answer sheets to help future students seeking a H.A.I.T. qualification. The following answer sheet, from candidate 008/717179/E/XZ/GROC of Wigan, was awarded an A+distinction & Diploma with a score of 93%.

Test Paper 1: Specimen 1

1. Emperor de Nero was unquestionably right to burn Rome because, as he later explained, it was part of an ongoing slum clearance scheme designed to reduce the risk of infection by disease-carrying rats, fleas, plebs & Roman mobs. Nevertheless responsible historians would have to admit that the policy turned out to be fatally unpopular for de Nero.

Queen Body Sear was also right to bum London. A known green conservationist, she intended to convert London into a brown site (although in the circumstances, it was more black than brown). The plan was to later restore it completely into a green site (after the embers had cooled). Of course the Romans, who had consistently refused to sign Kyoto, opposed this policy.

However, the Fizzy Goths should not have sacked Rome because it was civilised (unlike them) & contained many nice buildings. And anyway they were illegal immigrants. Their leader, Al Eric, seeking to justify it, referred to the famous 407 A.D. Barbarians Cup Final between them & the AstroGoths, a gripping event. The Fizzy Goths were winning 1-0 until the final 2 minutes of the game, but the Roman ref. then awarded two iffy penalties to the Astrogoths, & the final score was 2-1 to them, to the fury of the Fizzies. Incidentally, the Astrogoths were so-called because of their known interest in Space. The Astrogoths were thus infuriated when the Fizzygothic soccer hooligans called them "Space cadets", "Astronauts" & "Airheads".

2. (a) Apocalyptic (b) Epic (c) An increased interest in the sport of chariot racing, & a campaign to make it safer (d) ruinous (e) Good as de Nero in the film *Quo Vadis* (f) Unethically incestuous.

3. Undoubtedly the Ancient Brits perpetrated many spoofs to deceive the modern archyologists. As described in that excellent publication "History made easy", Silbeery hill was a good example of this, costing archyologists buckets of sweat & probably millions of man/woman hours for a result of precisely zero. The Brits probably did this because they did not relish the idea of being dug up, even 2,000 years later, & anyway it was against their religion.

4. (i) Atrocious certainly, but warming (ii) A long-established Brit tradition (iii) Colourful pictorially, but unreadable to anyone over twelve (iv) A true Brit heroin virago, possibly now re-incarnated in the person of Ann Widdecombe (v) O.K. on the weekends (vi) Do you mean Shrek? (vii) Also alright on the weekends.

5. Too gruesome to mention.

6. Because their motto was "Easy come, easy go".

7. Julia, in my opinion, was a woman transvestite with hermaphroditic tendencies, because when the Legions gave her the password "Who's a pretty boy, then?", they really meant it. Also it was known that he/she liked rough

trade, & it is thought that his killers, Brute & Cussius, were probably jealous ex-partners.

8. Yes, because they were right in thinking that this would benefit the tourist trade.

9. (i) Probably first said by Emperor Adrian when he sat on one of his stone toilets on Adrian's wall in a raging blizzard (ii) First said in the Pictish settlement of Glasgow on a Saturday night (iii) First said about the Paris mob by Queen Marie-Antoinette. She was a philosopher by profession (iv) Sid James to Kenneth Williams on the set of "Carry on Cleo".

10. Yes, in favour.

11. (a) Dangerous to pedestrians, especially lollipop men (b) A holy terror alias Jupiter (c) New fangled machines - throwing rocks is uncivilised, even on the battlefield (d) Too good at demolition (e) Teeth-gritting.

12. Stealth taxes had already been imposed on the Brit chariot owners who were forced to have road tax & insurance. So the answer to this is YES.

13. No, but it was certainly a crummy state according to Queen Body Sear, the Picts, the Scotch, the Anglos & the Saxons.

**

We have also provided specimen answer 2 as an example of how **NOT** to do it. The candidate had better remain nameless.

Test Paper 1: Specimen 2

1. Right - wrong - right. Okay?

2. Don't know any of 'em, but I think Ben Her might be a Scotch mountain (?).

3. I've seen stone hinge, & it's true - it's all ruined.

4. I don't know, I'm a Plymouth supporter. I also like page 3.

5. It will be short 'cos I don't know.

6. They should've joined BUPA.

7. I think he was an old hag, actually.

8. No.

9. The only one I know is getting legless.

10. What?

11. My uncle had a mangle wurzel, at least I think that's what it was. As for Scotch pipes, I don't smoke.

12. Yes.

13. Say what you like - we Brits don't care.

***

For more specimen answers, send a £5 Postal order & stamped / addressed envelope to A. Groper, 8 Rawalpindi Rd., Stornoway, Outer Hebrides.

CHAPTER 2
THE DARK AGES

THE LEGENDARY KING ARTHUR

After the Romans left Britain chaos ensued with invasions by the Picts & Scotch from the North, and more seriously, by Anglos & Saxons from the East. England clearly needed a legendary King. Luckily there happened to be a magical sword called Excalibre (sometimes X-calibre) embedded in a rock, which no-one could draw out unless they were legendary. The young Arthur had always been attracted to the idea of being legendary, so he tried it out and found he could draw it out easily. Unluckily however, Arthur accidentally dropped Excalibre into a nearby Lake. Luckily though, this particular lake had a legendary lady: "The Lady of the Lake" alias Lady Go-diver, who immediately dived in, being an expert diver, and fished up Excalibre[3].

---

[3] Lady Go-diver later became even more legendary by becoming the first female Naturalist, proving it by riding on a horse naked through the streets of Coventry (Lady G.-D. being naked, not the horse). This also gave rise to the English phrase "in Coventry", because after her exploit, no-one in Coventry would speak to her.

Arthur, now being the owner of Excalibre was immediately appointed King, and not just any King but a legendary King with a round table and a bunch of top knights. So Arthur built a legendary castle at Camalot, & gathered them round the round table to discuss his plans. He pointed out that all these invading Picts, Scotch, Anglos, Saxons & Jutes were illegal immigrants and trying to make England multicultural, and this had to stop. They all agreed that this would be a Good Thing, and so went off and fought many legendary battles which were all victories, naturally.

Sadly, though, in spite of all these triumphs, two of his best knights, Sir Lancalot & Sir Galabad ran off with his wife, Queen Gwinavear. Then, badly wounded by his legendary old enemy, Morbid, Arthur found himself by the sea with three old Queens. Luckily soon a boat arrived and carried Arthur off to the legendary island of Atlantis, which later sank beneath the waves, according to Pluto, thus becoming even more legendary, and Romantic to boot.

On the whole, however, King Arthur must be regarded as a Good Thing.

THE ANGLO-SAXON INVASION & SETTLEMENT

In spite of King Arthur and rough weather at sea, the Anglos & Saxons continued to sail across the North sea & invade, forcing the Brits & Romano Brits to move to Wales, where they became Welsh and stopped being English. Those who didn't like the Welsh had to move on to Cornwall, and those who didn't like the Cornish had to move on further to Brittinny in France, and had to become French, of course. Naturally, the Saxons now became the English. All this was obviously a good example of multiculturalism. Historians are undecided on whether this was A Good Thing, but they have all agreed that it was certainly politically correct!

The Anglos & Saxons travelled to England by boats called "Shortships", each carrying a knife called a Seax, which is why they were called Seaxons (or Sassafrass by the Scotch). On arrival on the English coast, they found that the Romans had considerately built them comfortable forts, called the Saxon shore.

No dates were recorded for these events as this was, of course, the Dark Ages and everyone was too busy fighting to record things. This was all left to a sensitive monk called the Vulnerable Bede.

THE DISADVANTAGES OF THE SAXONS & ANGLOS

Although the Saxons all wanted to become English, they had many disadvantages:-

1. They did not speak the language.

2. Being barbarians they were anti-Roman and did not maintain the Roman roads, cities and villas, which thus fell into ruins - more Urban Blight! (For the first example of this see under "Queen Body Sear's Rebellion: Getting Legless".)

3. They had far too many Kings who were always fighting and slaughtering each other, that is when they were not fighting and slaughtering the Brits, the Roman Brits, the Welsh, the Scotch, the Picts, the Irish & the French (& later, the Vikings & the Danes)! All these Kings invariably had impossible names starting with words like "Wolf" or "Ethel" and usually ending with "Bert" or "Fred" (e.g. Ethelbert & Wolfred - now "Wilfrid"). One of these awful Kings who was clearly eccentric, even got himself

buried in a boat, of all things. This was later discovered at Sutton, but because Archyologists were unable to find out the King's name, Sutton had to be renamed "Sutton Who?"

4. They were pagans, worshipping the Sun and Moon and many other gods from which we get our days of the week. It wasn't until St. Augustine arrived and converted them to being Church of England at Canterbury that they began to become English.

5. They invented a lot of vulgar 4-letter words, and some others which had more than 4 letters but were even **worse!**

Only two Saxon Kings were at all memorable the first being Pender, King of Marcia, who made financial reforms by inventing the Penny. Then there was Offer, who built a wall along the Welsh border called Offer's dyke to keep the Welsh out (or in, depending on your viewpoint).

LAWS

Due to Urban Blight (see above) the Saxons had no prisons, so they devised a payment system for crimes, called "Weird-gold". Murder was the most expensive, but you could choose cheaper crimes. This was a Good Thing because poor men could not afford crime, and so remained poor. At the same time, as only the rich could afford murder, you got a better class of murderer.

TRIALS

The Saxons had many types of trial:-

a. Trial by combat (fighting to the death) - a Good Thing because it immediately halved the criminal population.

b.   Trial by Ordure - by which suspects had to pick up some ordure from a cauldron of boiling water. Thus it was soon noticed that most criminals had one arm only.

c.   Witches were tried by dropping them in the river. If they sank they were innocent, though drowned of course. If they floated, they were guilty and burned at the steak. Thus the number of witches was rapidly reduced to zero (at least until the swimming certificate was introduced).

Another Good Thing the Saxons did was to introduce Meade, and even better, **Real Ale,** which they drank out of horns, skulls, hogsheads and firkins.

THE VIKINGS

By now, around 700 A.D. England was scheduled for another invasion and this was done by people called Vikings who were from many countries and were also called Northmen, Norsemen, Danes, Norwegians, Phatal Phalanxes, and even, occasionally, Swedes (the stupid ones).

One of the main reasons for their success was that they lived in long houses, sailed in long ships and did very long voyages in their long ships (e.g. to America). In fact everything they had was long, including even the long horns on their helmets which terrified their enemies who thought they were being charged by longhorn cows or bulls, or even handsome devils. Hence the old English expression "on the horns of a dilemma". Some of these Vikings, called Bare Shreks, sharpened their teeth and stripped off their shirts in battle to fight more ferociously (Bareshrekly) like the Man. U striker Vern Ronay.

Their leaders also had fierce names like Ragnad Hairy Breeches, Ernie Bloodaxe, Harold Hard-Rider, Ivan the Gormless, Kirk Douglas, Tony Curtis & Einar the Terrible.

The first Viking raids on England were not very serious as they only killed a couple of Aldermen, and raided monasteries for their gold. Much, much later Henry VIII solved this problem by dissolving all the monasteries & keeping all the gold for himself (see under "The Dissolution of the Dissolute Monasteries").

Later however these Vikings or Danes decided to get serious about invading. It is important to note that while in their longships, the Vikings were Vikings, but as soon as they landed anywhere they all became "Danes" instantaneously. Their main aim was to become English themselves, thus displacing the current English (Anglos & Saxons) - yet another example of Multiculturalism. It is not known what they planned to do with the existing English, but some think they wanted to drive them west into Wales (as the Saxons had done to the first English or Britons), and thus force them to become Welsh like the first English.

Under Ivar the Gormless and Half Dane, the Viking host invaded the East coast. It is important to understand that, like the Romans, the Vikings did not have "armies" but "hosts". Their first act was to kill all the English Kings - not a bad idea as there were far too many at the time. One of them was called Bury St. Edmund, who was buried conveniently at a town of the same name. It should be remembered that there were too many kingdoms too, e.g. Middle Sex, West Sex, East Sex (now more decently called Essex), East Anglia, West Anglia, North Humbria, Cumbria, Kent, Thanet, Merseyside, Marcia, Bernicia & Galicia, to name but a few.

After all this there was only one King left - Alfred (not yet the Great), who, though Saxon, was also very English, which was a Good Thing. Alfred managed to escape from the Great Danes by hiding in a bog on the island of Alderney, in the cottage of an old groan. One day she asked him to mind some cakes she had on the griddle while she popped down to the supermarket. But Alfred burned the cakes and was badly scolded by the groan. He then decided that domestic bliss was not for him, & he henceforth left Alderney (not to be confused with Avalon in the Channel islands), collected an army and defeated the Danes. This was such a Good Thing, that Alfred immediately became "THE GREAT".

Alfred was not an unkind man, however, & he told the Danes that they could stay in England provided they all moved north of Wotling street in the North East, and could become English provided they settled down and learned the language. He even allowed them to keep their loot (Danegold) and their law (Danelaw). Many thus became English (Northerners), and were even allowed to keep their atrocious accents. A few bad ones spent all their Danegold and started raiding again, remaining Danes (not a Good Thing)!

ALFRED THE GREAT

Alfred liked being "the Great" and so decided to continue this by:-

1. Becoming the **Only King of all England.** This was not too difficult as the Danes had already knocked off all the others.

2. Being Multicultural - A Good Thing.

3. He built the English Navy, cunningly making Longer ships than the Danish Longships, and thus defeated them again.

4. He ordered English townspeople to build burrows (boroughs) where they could hide if the Vikings or Danes came back.

5. He made a new regulation stating that from then on the English could have only one King at a time, which was of course himself.

6. He learned to read & write. This was extremely rare among royals around that time, and they usually got monks like the Vulnerable Bede to write their letters for them.

***

After Alfred, his son Edward Iron Teeth kept up the good work and made sure the English kept to the new regulation of one King only - himself. The next King, Applestan carried on the good work, but sooner or later, by the law of averages, there had to be a Bad King, and therefore a Bad Thing ...

ETHELREED THE UNRULY

Ethelreed was called "the Unruly" because, to save his life, he just could not rule. Some of the Danes who had refused to be multicultured into Englishmen, noticed this and tipped off their Viking relatives abroad. Together they plotted against the Unruly Ethelreed and started the first known protection racket in history. This worked as follows: each year they sailed to England and threatened to attack it unless Ethelreed bought them off with Danegold. Thus each year the King who was weak as well as being Unruly had to pay the Danes off until the next year when he would get another hefty bill.

As a result, Ethelreed hated the Danes so much that he decided to massacre all the Danes currently living in England. Unluckily for the Unruly, King Swine of Denmark heard about this scheme & so quickly invaded England and made his son the new King, driving Ethelreed into exile. Thus a Danish King called Knut, or "Nut" for short now ruled all England.

KING KNUT, OR "NUT" FOR SHORT

Nut was a good king but easily flattered, so when some of his courtiers told him he ruled the waves, he decided to prove them right. He took the courtiers down to his beachside palace, & had a crafty look at the tide tables, unknown to them. Thus later, on the beach, he sat in his deck chair and commanded those waves to go back, and as the tide had turned, THEY DID! But the effect was somewhat lost the next day, when a tsunami arrived and wrecked his beach palace. Luckily, Nut was already halfway back to London with his courtiers by that time.

EDWARD THE PROFESSOR

The next king was a saintly man called Edward the Professor. Unfortunately he had no children, being too saintly to engage in such matters. His one great achievement was to build Westminster Abbey, but he did precious little else.

But when Edward died the throne of England was more or less up for grabs & the contest was between three powerful men, Harold, William the Bastard & Harold Hard-Rider, as we shall see.

THE BATTLE OF HASTINGS AND ALL THAT

As Harold was a national hero, having won several wars, the English naturally chose him as their King. But William, Duke of Normandy said that Edward the Professor had promised him the throne instead, and that Harold was welshing on an oath to that effect. But the English didn't care as they didn't like William who was not a nice man, & because of this was called "The Bastard" and many other things as well, undoubtedly. Not only that, but he was French (!) & a Duc rather than a good English Duke. As for the Normans themselves, they were just recycled Vikings who had multicultured themselves into Frenchmen (what bad taste!).

To make matters worse, another Harold was interested, although he was being greedy as he was already King of Norway. This was Harold Hard-Rider, a Viking.

1066

Harold Hard-Rider got the ball rolling by invading the North, but King H. promised him just 6 feet of English soil & then defeated him. So the Viking host lost away at Stamford bridge - Scratch one Harold!

While this was going on Duc William had sneakily landed at Hastings behind Harold's back, in his usual underhand way. On arrival he fell down on the sand and ate a handfull of it to prove he was the real King of England. (This particular habit never caught on with subsequent English Kings - I wonder why?)

Harold arrived back at Hastings in due course, but his army was pretty knackered as it is hard work defeating a

Viking host, let alone marching all the way up the country & then all the way down it again.

The English lined up on a hill with a hairy apple tree at a place conveniently called Battle. They fought behind a shield wall, and the tactics were simply to clobber anything which came within range with their long axes. At first this worked well as the Norman knights kept riding up the hill and duly clobbered. But the English had no calvary or archers & soon the wily William used an underhand trick - he told his men to pretend to run away. This lured the English pheasants ("the feared") to break ranks and chase. They were soon wiped out by the dastardly Normans.

William also noticed that the shield wall had walls but no roof. So he told his bowmen to shoot high. This worked well, and we all know the rest of the story. The good King Harold got an arrow in the eye, the English lost heart and ran away. The battle was lost: Scratch two Harolds. William 2, the Harolds nil.

Thus William the Bastard Duc became William the Conquistador & King of England. Poor Harold was the last King of the English who was actually English, R.I.P.

All of this was commemorated in the famous Bayonne tapestry, although no-one knows who actually made it.

WILLIAM THE CONQUISTOR

After his victory at Hastings, William the Conquistador ravaged England from end to end - the correct action for all aspiring Conquistadors. Thus he became known as the Conquistor, or more often "The Bastard". Also this proved to the English who was the boss from now on, & how Norman civilisation worked.

As he was now a full King & not just a Duck (of Normandy), William decided to make a lot of changes - something that was easy enough as Parliament had not yet been invented, and so there was no-one to argue. These changes were bad but IMPORTANT, & therefore A GOOD THING:-

1. He ruled that from now (1066) the only REAL ENGLISH were the Normans (who had already been Vikings, & then French). This was because they were now the RULING CLASS, and thus multicultural. As for Harold's English, they were no longer "English" & were demoted to being Saxons again, or even Anglos, & not only that, but just pheasants (see later under "Robbing Hood").

2. That from then on (1066) all future Kings or Queens of England must be Foreign, except of course the Normans who were now English! They could be French, Welsh, Scotch, Dutch, Hybrid (e.g. Queen Anne) or even German (The Hunnoverians & Sack-Coalbags[4]), with even the odd Greek thrown in. This was because until then all previous Kings had been English & therefore it would only be fair to give foreigners a go, in the interests of multiculturalism. This rule has always been observed, & therefore must have been a Good Thing.

3. From then on all Kings & Queens must have not only a name, but a NUMBER, & most importantly DATES. This

---

[4] During World War I the Royal Family decided that it would not be a Good Thing to continue as Germans (Sack-Coalbags), & so instantly changed into Englishmen (& women) by becoming Winsors after the very popular (& English) castle, brown soup & tie knot. Their cousins, the Batterburgers did likewise, becoming The Montbatons, & thus very popular & good too!

was very significant because it started REAL HISTORY & ended the Dark Ages.

THE FEWDALL (OR FUTILE) SYSTEM

William made one very important invention: The Fewdal or Futile system. This stated a lot of v. significant new rules:-

a.   Absolutely Everything in England now belonged to the King, i.e. him, William. Anyone who didn't like it was doomed, as he wrote in his Doomsday book, which was usually true.

b.   His Norman (now English) supporters must build castles all over England, and oppress the pheasants. If they did this well, he would make them Earls, Ducks, Barons, Lords or Knights, and they could eat the fat of the land, drink & be merry. This of course was the origin of that wonderful institution, The House of Lords.

c.   All Saxons (& Anglos) must now become pheasants and work on the land from dawn till dusk. This even applied to those who had held other jobs before 1066.

d.   Pheasants were divided into different types for easy recognition. These were: (i) Surfs (very clean pheasants) (ii) Villains (very bad pheasants) (iii) Soakmen (very drunk pheasants - hence the saying "an old soak") & (iv) Yeomen, who would later become bowmen.

This system was consequently often called "Bastard Fewdalism" for obvious reasons.

Finally, in order to give the Saxons an even harder time, he put up England's first purpose-built prison, the Tower of London (which proved very useful to many other Kings & Queens later (especially Richard III, Henry VIII & Broody Mary)).

He also passed the Gaming laws to prevent the pheasants from gambling, & finally a curfew so that the pheasants could not go out after dark, gaming, binge-drinking, or even hunting deer, which of course, all belonged to Him, William.

Saxons who obeyed all this were in-laws & miserable, but those who didn't became outlaws & were Merry men (see under "Robbing Hood").

When William died he was buried in Rowan cathedral (which can still be seen) in France. Thus he set up a new tradition of English Kings being buried in France (see under "The Middle Ages").

OTHER NORMAN KINGS

There were three other Norman, or English Kings. The first was William II, or William Rufus or "Roughouse", who was called this because he had red hair & a red nose, & liked brawls, or roughouses in pubs. Rufus was not popular, and one day out hunting in Sherwood forest with his friends he was shot by an arrow at a place called Stormy Cross. (So much for friendship!) One of his friends Sir Walt Tiler (not to be confused with Wot Toiler, the Pheasant - see next chapter under "The Wars of the Roses") was accused of this dastardly crime. But Sir Walt denied it, saying it had been done by a man dressed all in green with a funny hat with a feather in it, called Robbing Hood. But no-one had yet heard of Robbing Hood, which they called a figment of Sir Walt's imagination, & anyway most probably legendary to boot, and so Sir Walt was banished.

The next two Kings, Henry I & Stephen are even less significant, being unpopular to boot. England was in chaos at the time because the barons had built too many castles all over the place & liked fighting each other. Thus many of the castles became dilapidated (more Urban Blight!).

Historical Aptitude & Intelligence Test
Test Paper 2: The Dark Ages
(1 hour 30 mins)

N.B. The same rules apply as in Test Paper 1.

1. Discuss early examples of Urban Blight, with reference to: (a) Queen Body Sear of the Icky tribe (b) Saxons (c) Norman Barons.

2. Was King Arthur really true, or just legendary? Be exact.

3. Discuss early feminism with reference to Lady Go-Diver. Was she a pioneer in the field or just a maverick exhibitionist? Try to avoid innuendo.

4. Why was a swimming qualification essential to Anglo-Saxon witches? Was this politically correct?

***

Multiple Choice Section:-

Tick either A, B, C, or D (but not all four!) & give a brief explanation.

5. Which of the following was clearly in breach of the Geneva Convention:

    a. Long ships

    b. Longer ships

    c. Long Axes

    d. Long Johns

6. Was William I a Bastard because:

    a. He beat up King Harold

    b. He beat up the English

    c. He beat up the pheasants

    d. All three of the above

7. Fill in the blanks in the following Anglo-Saxon words:

    a. _u _ _

    b. _ _c _

    c. F_ _ _

    d. _ _ _ _ _ _y

    N.B. This question should NOT be attempted by candidates of a nervous disposition, in Holy orders or under 10 years of age!

***

8. With reference to the burning of the cakes, was Alfred the Great, or the Grate?

9. Explain the meaning of the following terms: (a) Going Bare Shrek (b) Sutton Who? (c) Trial by ordure (d) Bastard feudalism (or futilism).

10. What made William I such an absolute Bastard?

THE END!

CHAPTER 3
THE MIDDLE AGES

A s the Normans had muffed things up so badly, it was only fair to let the French have a go at being Kings of England. Henry II was the first of these, and he spent most of his time in France with his French wife, Eleanor of Acetone (a part of France). He also followed William I's multicultural example, by dying & being buried there. Henry was a good & strong King, according to all the historians, although it is not altogether clear why.

Henry had one good friend & boom companion called Thomas R. Bucket, (or Bouquet in French) who was also, strangely enough, a Saxon. As a compliment to R. Bucket the King made him Archbishop of Canterbury. But Thomas took advantage of this by becoming a saint (St. Thomas R. Bucket), which was decidedly **not** what Henry had in mind at all. Furthermore, when Henry told Bucket that he wanted the Church in England to become C. of E. with him, Henry, as its chief instead of the Pope, Thomas said no dice, which made Henry even angrier.

In a rage, the King complained to some of his knights, saying, "Who will rid me of this tumorous priest?" Not surprisingly, the knights took this as a heavy hint, & donning their armour they set out to solve this problem by killing poor St. Thomas R. Bucket in the cathedral. Henry was full of remorse about this, and so cut up about it that he made a pilgrimage to Canterbury dressed only in his nightshirt, & ordered the monks there to whip him. The knights concerned were of course banished forthwith. The whole incident is historically very important as it led to pilgrimages, the Canterbury tails, Geoffrey Chawcer (who was a good riter although probably one of the wust spellers in histry), murder in the cathedral, & in more recent times even Peter O'Toole & Richard Burton.

RICHARD THE LOINHEART & JOHN

Richard the Loinheart was the next king. He was good, but unusually absent, as he had started a new war called the crusades against the fierce Sarcens in the Holy, & unholy places. These Sarcens were led by a ferocious lady called Sally Dinn (or Djinn) who had many battles with Richard which neither side won. So eventually, getting fed up with an inconclusive war, Richard set off for home, but was kidnapped & locked up by the treacherous Emperor of Australia, who probably didn't like Poms.

Luckily a passing minstrelle called Blondie found out about this. She took the news back to England with instructions to Prince John to raise a ransom a.s.a.p. Prince John had been left in charge of England as Richard was so absent.

Prince John was an evil, greedy prince who later became an evil greedy king. He began collecting money for the ransom by taxing everybody, including the barons. The only way to evade these taxes was to become an outlaw & go to live with Robbing Hood & his Merry men in Sherwood New Forest (see under "Robbing Hood"). Meanwhile, having collected enough money to ransom his brother Richard, John being typically greedy & selfish, decided to keep it for himself instead.

This annoyed the barons who rose against John & took him to Running Mead, a swamp near London, & refused to let him out of the mud until he agreed to sign a big poster called the Magner Poster. This poster promised Englishmen many new liberties, which they often took, and is thought by many historians to be a GOOD THING[5].

Meanwhile, the Emperor of Australia, realising he was not going to get his ransom, released King Richard, grumbling that he was eating him out of castle & home, & muttering about "stingy Poms". Luckily for John, Richard did not come back to England, but went & joined yet another war in France, where he was shot by an arrow by a French pheasant. Of course it was strictly against the laws of wars as pheasants were only supposed to kill other pheasants, not barons or kings. Only barons & kings could kill barons & kings, not pheasants, though of course, the barons & kings **could** also kill pheasants too. So when the French pheasant claimed that he had thought that Richard was just another English pheasant, it was brought to his notice that pheasants did not normally wear suits of full plate armour stamped with gold carrots & with crowns on their helmets!

---

[5] As the only English were the ruling class (i.e. barons), the Saxon pheasants were not included in these new liberties, and so could still be oppressed, and indeed should be!

None of this however did Richard any good, as he was dead & that was that!

ROBBING HOOD

At about this time Robin Hood, or "Robbing Hood" as the rich called him, was a legendary[6] outlaw who lived in the New Sherwood forest with his Merry men, including Long John, Fryer Turk, Will Starlet, & of course his girlfriend, Maid Marlene.

Robin & his Merry men made a living redistributing wealth by robbing from the rich and giving it to the poor, that is to say the in-laws or poor Saxon pheasants, who, not being outlaws were miserable, unlike the outlaws who were always Merry. But Robin did not give all the money away, as he had to keep his men Merry at all times.

He dressed in Lincoln green, with a funny hat & was a crack shot with a bow and arrows, as the Sharif of Nottingham found out to his cost. Among other things (like Normans), he also shot deer in the forest which was, of course, forbidden to in-laws, thus providing his Merry men with fresh meat at all times. His men were also dead shots with their bows, at least when they weren't too Merry.

There are many Romantic tales of Robin's deeds which should not be repeated in a serious history like this, as they are legendary!

As he lay dying, Robin fired an arrow through his bedroom window into the forest outside, telling his men, who for once weren't Merry, to bury him wherever the arrow fell, but

---

[6] Being legendary means that he may not have been true, but on the other hand he may have been.

sadly they never found the arrow, & so Robin had to be buried in an unmarked grave.

Incidentally, the New Sherwood forest is now also legendary, having been redeveloped by wealthy Typhoons. So the rich got the last laugh after all!

***

Meanwhile, the greedy & evil King John was still being greedy & evil in spite of the Magna Poster. However Fate was against him, and he lost his entire treasure in a Tsunami in the Wash, an early example of money laundering.

Not surprisingly, John died of a broken heart and a surfeit of Lampoons.

PARLIAMENT (PRON. "PAR-LEE-AY-MENT")

The next King, Henry III was dull and uninteresting, had favourites and was a wimp. So a French baron called Simon de Mountford decided to solve this problem by inventing parliament. This is thought to have been a GOOD THING by all except the next King, Edward the Hammer, who abolished both parliament and Simon de Mountford in a single battle at Evesham. So that was that, at least for the time being.

EDWARD I "THE HAMMER"

Having hammered Simon de Mountford & parliament, Edward looked around for something else to hammer. So first he decided on the Welsh, who put up a good fight but got hammered. To keep them hammered, Edward then built castles all over Wales and made his eldest son "Prince of Wales", which can be seen today, the castles that is, not the Prince.

A SCOTCH PROBLEM

Edward soon discovered that, like the Romans before him, he had a Scotch problem, & decided to solve it by hammering the Scotch. This he did again & again, but still the Scotch stubbornly refused to be English, or even British, or to give up their strange & hideous customs.

Since the Romans had built Adrian's wall to keep the Scotch in, they had refused to become either Roman, Saxon (Sassafras), Viking, Norman, British or even English. They had very strange habits, wore skirts but no knickers, threw telephone poles around & blew into the bag making very strange noises indeed. Their eating habits defy description, but at least they invented whisky (but not Bourbon which was French, of course). All this was extremely distressing to the English, but Edward proved that any amount of hammering didn't improve the situation, so he died.

EDWARD II & THE HAMMERING SCOTCH PROBLEM (CONT.)

Unlike his father the 1st, Edward, the 2nd one, was a weak man who had favourites, and was thus unpopular, especially with the barons who suspected him of being gay, & wanted to keep on hammering the Scotch, as they had acquired a taste for it. But, alas, those stubborn Scotch decided to do a bit of hammering themselves, and so won two big battles & thus hammered the English themselves[7].

The first of these battles was at Starling bridge where the Scotch were led by a national hero, Wallace Williams. (This at least is what historians call him, but everyone knows that

---

[7] This was unusual & went against the usual Scotch custom of losing all their battles against the Romans & English. But they found this new tactic equally effective, & much more satisfying.

his real name was Mal Gibson.) But Wallace's victory was unfair & only **half** a victory as only half the English army had crossed the bridge, & so only half got wiped out. The other half sensibly stayed on their own side of the river, & complained it was unfair & against the rules.

But the second Scotch victory was a **whole** victory, by King Robert the Bruse (Scotch for "bruiser"). King Robert, like Alfred the Great, had a checkered early career, spending much of his time hiding in caves counting spiders. Before the battle, the English sent forward their Heavy-knight Champion Shrek der Bohunk (or Bohulk), but the Bruiser whacked him with his war hammer & said: "I hereby declare you well & truly Hammered!" So, not surprisingly, this brought on the famous Battle of Bannock Bun, near O Bun. The Scotch had, rather unfairly, dug pits into which all the English knights duly fell, & were thus thoroughly defeated. The final straw for them was the appearance of a mob of Glasgow Celtic soccer hooligans on the hill behind the Scotch army all chanting wild things like "Scotch way hay" & "There ye gae, there ye gae, there ye gae / There ye gae, there ye gae, there ye gae-eee!" ect. Terrified by this uncouth spectacle, the English vacated Scotland precipitously. This meant the Scotch could continue to be Scotch & keep the Scone of Stone.

Poor Edward II was blamed for all this, & was thus put to death in a gruesome way by some gruesome barons. Thereby he started a new custom followed by many weak English Royals, & even Pretenders, of being murdered in dark & gloomy dungeons of dark & gloomy castles (e.g. Richard II, Henry VI, the Princes in the Tower, the Duke of Claridges (a wino), Parkin Wartbeck, Lady Joan Grey, Mary Queen of Scotch, ect., ect. ...).

THE HUNDRED YEARS WAR

The next Edward (the III or "Third time lucky") sensibly decided to change tactics & **not** hammer the Scotch, as it clearly did no good. So he looked around for someone else to hammer, & after some thought, decided the French would be ideal. Having made this important decision he declared war on them for 100 years, to show he really meant it, & invaded France forthwith.

Before going further, it should be explained that the English pheasants now had a revolutionary new weapon, the Longbow. This had actually been first invented by the Welsh in Cardiff Arms Park. In spite **of** this the longbow proved **to** be very successful since it could shoot farther & faster than the short bow, or even the Crossbow. But Edward realised he would have to change the rules **of** war, so he explained **to** his pheasants that they could now shoot knights & nobles (& even Kings), just so long as they were **French** knights & nobles (& even Kings), & **NOT** English knights & nobles (or even Kings)!

This was all very important & significant, as will be seen later.

THE BATTLE OF CRESSY

Thus Edward won a very important victory at Cressy. This was because the Goanese crossbowmen were very cross because they had to wind up their crossbows every time they shot an arrow, whereas the English longbows were fully automatic, & so much faster. Moreover the Goanese crossbowmen got even crosser when the French knights galloped right over them, & walked off the job back to Goa. Being multicultural, Edward had a Black prince who did well in the battle & won his spares (he had a dodgy set of armour), & generally a great time was had by all. But, of course, the French showed bad sportsmanship by complaining that the English shouldn't have let their pheasants shoot nobles (& even Kings) as this was against the rules. But the English thumbed their noses & raised two fingers, pointing out that one of their Kings, Richard I, had been shot by a French pheasant years earlier, so there! It is thought that another new invention, the cannon, was used at Cressy as many large balls have been found there. Of course, as is well known, gunpowder had already been invented by an immigrant Chinese monk called Roger Bai Coon.

Of course, Edward won many more important & glorious victories, all of which are memorable The French also won the occasional victory too, but these are not memorable, being French, & are now largely forgotten (at least, by the English).

THE WARS OF THE ROSES

Richard II started as a strong & brave young king. He settled the pheasants' revolt by killing their leader, Wot Toiler in cheapside & sending the revolting pheasants home. But later he allowed the Wars of the Roses, & became a weak king, which was asking for trouble at the time.

Meantime, 2 noble families, one from Yorkshire & the other from Lancs, quarrelled over which was better, white roses or red roses. Despite arbitration by the Yorks & Lancs meddyeval rose-growers associations, war inevitably broke out. The matter was resolved (for a time) by one of the Lancs men, Bollsinbroke, who deposed Richard II & became a strong king, Henry IV part I. Richard II continued the time-honoured custom of weak kings by being murdered in a very dark dungeon of a very dark castle.

Although a strong king, Henry IV part I was uneasy. Being afraid his crown might be stolen he kept it on in bed & thus suffered headaches & insomnia. Desperate, the King changed from Henry IV part I to Henry IV part II, which immediately solved the problem.

Meanwhile, his eldest son was the memorable, but dissolute, Prince Hal, later to become the even more memorable and strong Henry V, a good king (but with a very bad wig). Prince Hal had misspent his youth with ageing rakes like False Stuff, a fat old man who drank sherry all day out of a sack; Buttolph, who had a large blue luminous nose like a lampoon; Pistol, who had a large one; & 2 fast ladies, Mistress Quicker & her daughter, Miss Quickest.

But, when he was crowned Henry V, Hal decided to become a Good King. "Get thee to a nunnery," he told his disreputable friends. False Stuff, Buttolph, Pistol & the 2 fast girls. The men were glad to do so, but the girls less so.

THE 100 YEARS WAR (CONT.)

Henry now decided to remind the French that 100 years had not elapsed since Edward III had started the 100 yrs. war, so they'd better watch out. Arriving in France he attacked Harf-hour by filling up his breeches with his English dead & making a rousing speech, thus memorably & successfully capturing the town. This was, of course, a Good Thing.

But Henry was not finished yet. He went on to win the v. famous & memorable Battle of A Gin Court. Using the same tactics as his predecessor Edward III, he massacred the flare of the French nobility, including a Chief Constable. The French later complained about this but got the usual English 2 fingers.

THE END OF THE 100 YEARS WAR

Sadly A Gin Court was the last English victory of the hundred years war - all the rest were French, & therefore instantly forgettable. At the end of the 100 years, the English had lost all their French possessions, largely *due* to an active working girl called Joan of Ark, a transvestite milkmaid, who also became a Saint. This was completely unfair to the manly English soldiers who refused to fight a girl, especially a girl Saint, so they lost. But poor St. Joan was then tried for hideousy & burnt at the steak, so France was given to a Dolphin. It is therefore very doubtful if the 100 years war was A Good Thing.

THE END OF THE WARS OF THE ROSES

A Welshman named Henry Tudor decided to end the Flower wars, & so he invented a new Rose which was both white & red at the same time, & this stopped the argument. Henry then collected an army for one last battle against the king, Richard III. Richard had been a dastardly king who had killed off many of his relatives like the Duke of Claridges who was drowned in a cask of his Mumsy's wine, & the Princes in the towers of course. The two armies met at Boswell, but Richard's men instantly deserted to the other side. Though dastardly, Richard was a brave man & continued to fight after hanging his crown on a hawthorn bash. Finally he tried to trade his kingdom for a horse - an early example of horse trading. Henry Tudor now declared that the next kings *(& queens)* of England would be Welsh, & he would be the first one called Henry VII.

He also decreed that the Middle Ages were OVER! (Thank God.)

Historical Aptitude & Intelligence Test
Test Paper 3: The Middle Ages
(1 hour 30 mins)

1. Compare & contrast in-laws & outlaws with careful reference to Robbing Hood, Maid Marlene & Fryer Turk.

2. Why did King John take so many liberties, & what was the object of the Magna Poster?

3. Was Parliament a good invention? Be honest!

4. Did the Scotch Hammer the English or was it the other way round?

5. Discuss the careers of Robert the Bruiser & Wallace Williams. Were they against the Geneva Convention?

6. Why did the French get 2 fingers? Was this also a breach of the Geneva Convention?

7. Write briefly on the importance of each of the following: (a) The Longbow (b) The short bow (c) The Crossbow (d) Bell bottoms (e) Cannon balls.

8. Why was Henry the VII?

9. Draw a colour-coded sketch map of the Battle of Cressy, putting in the cross Goanese crossbowmen, the shortbowmen, the longbowmen, the Black prince & any other natural features *you* can think of.

10. Why were the French unfair in using Saint Joan against the English? Could this be called a war crime?

THE END!

H.A.I.T. Test Paper 3:
Model Answer Specimen

1. In-laws were always miserable pheasants who were oppressed by Norman barrens & were not allowed to hunt deer, or even go gaming in the woods. But the out-laws like Robbing Hood were always very Merry men, who also each had a Merry Maid like Merry Maid Marlene & Little Joan. Fryer Turk was a fat fryer who, being fat was not so much "Merry" as "Jolly".

2. King John took all freeborn Englishmen's liberties, but the Magna Poster put an end to this by forbidding him to do so, & condemning him to a surfeit of Lampoons, & a Typhoon in the Wash (money-laundering).

3. This is highly debatable ... highly debatable.

4. The Scotch undeniably did the most hammering as Bravehurt (Mal Gibson) defeated them at Stallion bridge, & Robert the Bruiser hammered the English Knight Heavyweight champion with his war hammer at Bannock bun in the O bun.

5. Covered in Q.4, okay?

6. This was the V-sign later made famous by Winston Churchill. The French got it because they were constantly complaining for a hundred years about the English pheasants & long bowmen.

7. (a) The Longbow was a traditional English weapon, invented by the Welsh, look you. (b) The shortbow was a traditional French weapon & therefore no good. (c) The Crossbow was so-called because it made its operatives wind it up before each shot, & that naturally made them

cross. (d) I dunno, but Bow bells is where cockneys come from. (e) Invented by the Chinese.

8.   I don't know why Henry was VII, but I do know why Henry was the VIII - because he had VIII wives, none of which survived the experience.

9.   See overleaf.

10. Of course, no soldier wants to fight sainted transvestite milk-maids in plate armour, or dolphins come to that, which was unfair & quite possibly a war crime to boot.

CHAPTER 4
THE TUDORS

HENRY VII

Henry Tudor, having invented the Tudor rose, which was both white & red, thus abolished the Wars of the Roses utterly & declared them null & void & absolutely forbidden & defunct. He also abolished the Middle Ages & made himself King Henry VII by conquest (see under "The End of the Wars of the Roses"), and by Parliamentary & popular consent, or else!

Luckily most of the British nobility had been wiped out by the Rose Wars, but Henry wanted to deal with the surviving ones, so he made it illegal for them to have private armies & castles & as they all did, he then took them to the Stir Chamber[8] where he fined them all so heavily that they had to start living on Livery & Maintenance.

Henry was plagued however by an outbreak of Pretenders who pretended to be one, or both the Princes in the Tower.

---

[8] So-called because if you did not pay your fine you would be put in Stir which was medieval slang for being locked up ... or worse.

What the actual Princes thought of this is not recorded for obvious reasons.

The first of these Pretenders, Perkin Wartback, was executed, that being the normal thing for pretenders at that time. But the second, Lambeth Simnel, coincided with a staff shortage in the Palace kitchen, so Henry thriftily gave him a job washing dishes & stalls (a stallion). Later the boy graduated to chef & was the origin of the famous, or infamous, Simnel cake.

Henry, being very thrifty & miserly, was probably the only known King to make an actual profit out of a war, by sending an array to France with no intention of actually fighting. He then threatened the cowardly French King, or Dolphin, with yet another Hundred years war unless he forked out. The French Dolphin did not suss the bluff, & paid a large sum of money and a field covered in clods of gold for the Brits to leave, which they did. Thus Henry invented the original protection racket, or in modern parlance PROTECTIONISM.

Henry was thus very good at making money, & left England a rich country. His son, Henry VIII was even better at spending this money which he did very quickly, & then raised more by degaussing the coinage with bass metal & dissolving dissolute monasteries, to say nothing of nunneries.

HENRY VIII OR "GRUFF KING HAL"

Unlike his dad, Henry VIII was a magnificent figure - very large, square & bluff. According to his portrait by Hens Holbuns he was also an extremely flashy dresser, with a remarkably large (or "flashy") coldpiece which demonstrated his prowess with the ladies, including, of course, his VIII wives. With his enormous square body & equally enormous square head, his appearance was described by the French ambassador as "Formidable". So large, in fact, that he had to have all the privies in the Palace rebuilt to accommodate his massive hulk. Hence the origin of the Olde English expression: "Built like a Bricke Shytte House".

WIVES

One (or 8) of Henry's most notable achievements was, as is well known, of marrying VIII wives in that order, most of whom were called Catherine (or Catharine, or Katharine or Katherine). Midway between his marrying career there was a slight lapse towards Annes (or Anns), but the King soon got fed up with them & reverted to Catherines.

These wives soon discovered that marriage to this Right Royal Hulk was not much fun, usually ending in divorce, or something rather more lethal. Henry's invariable excuse for divorce (or worse) was that he needed a son to avoid a Feminist Queen, & so far be only had II daughters: By Our Lady Mary & the Virgin Faery Queen, or Glory Anna, Elizabeth. His Ist wife was Katherine of Avalon, an important part of Spain. But more of this later.

CARDINAL WOOLLY

Henry's Ist chief minister was an apprentice Pope called Woolly. It was scurrilously suggested that Cardinal Woolly was "sprung from humble origins" as a Lancashire wool carder (or cardigan), hence his name. Woolly soon became very rich & powerful, but this attracted more scurrilous gossip - that he was guilty of nepotism (favouring his nieces), simony (being simple-minded), leechery (being ad-dicted to leeches), pluralism (having more than one wife), polygamy (having more than one parrot) & numerous other unspeakable abuses. But Woolly disregarded all this & built himself the famous red brick Palace of Hamden court, complete with spacious red brick privies for Royal visits. Hence the Olde English expression "red brick amenities".

Meanwhile the Bluff King had grown fed up with his Ist wife, Katherine of Avalon, who had only had a daughter (see under "By Our Lady (or Bl__y) Mary") & had fallen in love with a comely young lady-in-waiting called Ann Boleyn (or Anne Boleyne). Not unnaturally, Henry wanted a divorce, so he sent Cardinal Woolly, a pal of the Pope, to Rome to get the divorce papers signed. Unfortunately for Woolly, the Pope wasn't having any & so inevitably Woolly fell. Luckily however for Henry, Archbishop Crammer suggested another solution: Sack the Pope, become Aprostrate, divorce Katherine of Avalon & marry Ann. Just like that. So England became a Prostratant country & the Pope was extirpated. Thus Henry made England from a R.C. country into C. of E., a Good Thing (?).

Henry's IInd wife Ann Boleyn produced another daughter. However, she soon grew tired of Hal's Bluff, & called it by having a lover. Not surprisingly, she died on the bloke, in spite of pleading that she had only been doing "a little necking".

THE RESTORATION (PROSTRATANTISM)

The first Prostratant was a German called Martin Luther (not King). Luther was a monk who was tired of celery (not being allowed to have a wife, or even a girlfriend) & so pinned 21 Thethes on the door of Wartenburg church. The infuriated Pope responded by sending a Bull, but Luther refusing to be "Bullied", burnt the Bull (not an especially easy thing to do, particularly if the Bull is uncooperative). In revenge Luther was tried by the Pope & Charles V, the un-

Holy, unRoman Emperor & condemned to solitary confinement on a Diet of Worms. But Luther was not perturbed & spent his time in the cooler translating the Bible from Latin into a new language called the Vernacular, & changing the word Prostratant into "Protestant", thus cleverly solving a spelling problem for future historians.

***

Meanwhile Henry was being persuaded to marry again by his advisers who showed him an attractive pin-up of the "Fair Maid of Flanders", Anne of Chives. But when he saw Anne in the flesh, he saw that he had been nobbled & declared rudely that she was **not** the "Fair Maid of Flanders" but the "Fat Mare of Flanders", & shipped her back in a cattle boat (for a previous example of horse-trading, see under "The End of the Wars of the Roses"). As for the advisers, he reduced them all by a head, as per usual for such people. After that Henry reverted to V more Catherines, making a grand total of VIII, of whom only the VIIIth survived being either divorced, beheaded or died!

THE DISSOLUTION OF THE DISSOLUTE MONASTERIES

Henry VIII was extravagant, not only in expensive clothes & wives (which are always expensive), but also in fighting more battles with the Scotch, which he won, & fighting wars with the French, which he didn't, but also in building unsinkable warships that immediately sank (e.g. the Merry Rose).

Thus, needing yet more money, Henry decreed that as all the monasteries were dissolute, they would be dissolved completely, & the land sold. Commissioners were sent all over the country with the difficult task of dissolving monasteries, but history does not record exactly how this was done. This left the monks & Fryers out of a job, but at least they had the consolation of being allowed to grow their hair, & even get married, & as there were now plenty of nuns available, this was not difficult!

Henry was also famous for building a new Navy with guns. One of his ships was called the Merry Rose, which sailed out to attack the French but soon sank without any assistance from the enemy, probably because of a loose cannon. Quite recently Prince Charles dug up the Merry Rose & made it into a museum which can still be seen today. Another of Henry's ill-fated ships, the Merry Celeste, entirely lost its crew in mysterious circumstances, which is why sailors are so superstitious.

THE RENUISSANCE

By this time, of course, Christobel Columbus, a Goanese Spaniard explorer, had correctly discovered America. Although the Vikings had already been there, they had incorrectly named it Wineland, & so their discovery has been ruled incorrect by all reputable historians. This important discovery proved that the World is round, & Columbus correctly named it "The Indies".

In Europe a new movement called the Renuissance had grown up, mainly in Italy, & then spread, even eventually to Britain. This movement was mainly about Humanism & ending the Middle Ages by copying the Ancient Romans & Greeks. This was of course a Good Thing.

Most of the Renuissance men were artists or sculptures or architects ect. One of the most famous was Leonardo der Vinchy who was mainly a painter who painted most parts of the body, inside & out! He also invented the first helicopter & many other machines. Another was the great Michael Angelo, a sculpture who also painted on the ceilings of chapels like the Cistern chapel in Rome - not an easy thing to do.

There were also Renuissance Kings, & Henry VIII was one of them. All these new Renuissance Kings had:-

1. Strong armies (to keep their barrens down).

2. Cannons (to knock the barrens castles down).

3. Strong Nationalism.

4. All read the celebrated Irish/Italian Renuissance writer Macky Avelli who told them to be **Ruthless.**

All this was an exceptionally Good Thing.

EDWARD VI

When Henry VIII died there were only 3 Tudors left. The first of these was Edward VI who was just a boy when he became King, & a sickly one at that. Thus he had to have 2 Lord Protectives, each of whom worked for 3 years & was then executed - the customary fate of such men. So, running out of Protectives after only 6 years, Edward himself died of consummation, leaving only 2 more Tudors, both of whom were girls.

BY OUR LADY (OR BL__Y) MARY

At this time there was also a pretender, pretending to be the real Queen, Lady Zane Grey. But she didn't last & was dispatched in the usual way.

Bl__y Mary was not so much Bl__y as Sooty, as will be seen. She was an R.C. & hated her Pa, Henry for becoming an Aprostrate & divorcing her Ma, Katherine of Avalon. She thus wanted revenge on the C. of E., whom she rudely called "Hairy Ticks". So she burned all the Hairy Tick Bishops &

Archbishops at the steak, including Crammer, who had put Henry up to the divorce, & many others. A man called Fox wrote a book about this called the Book of Martyres, but of course Mary banned publication. However some sarcastic composer wrote a song called "Keep the home fires burning!"

In order to have a hair, Mary married Philip of Spain, but still could not have a hair & so died of a broken heart which had "calamity" written on it. Altogether Mary should not be regarded as a Good Thing, & this left just one more Tudor only.

ELIZABETH I, THE VIRGIN QUEEN A.K.A. THE FAERIE QUEEN A.K.A. GLORY ANNA

Elizabeth I was a virgin as she never married in her life, but was the last of the Tudors as she had no hairs. She also started the Golden Age. She had many suitors for marriage, including the Dolphin of France & Sir Walter Raleigh, who lay down in a puddle so she could walk across with dry feet. Perhaps some of the suitors were put off when she told her soldiers that she had the heart & stomach of a King.

Unlike B. Mary, Elizabeth was C. of E. so all the R.C.s left in England were now the hairy ticks & had to hide their priests in holes, only letting them out for secret Masses.

WAR WITH SPAIN

Elizabeth had to have a war with Spain because the King, Philip, was an R.C. & B. Mary's Ex, & also because he burned a lot of Protestants in Autos de Fee. At that time the R.C.s had a thing called the Inquisitive which burned Hairy Ticks, & if they couldn't lay their hands on any, they burned smutty books instead. Philip was also annoyed because English pirates like

Francis Drake were robbing his treasure ships & taking the loot back to England to give to the Queen, which was why it was called the Golden Age. Elizabeth of course was very pleased with this & she gave all the pirates special licences & told them that from now on they were not so much pirates as "Privatears" which was much more respectable.

FRANCIS DRAKE

Francis Drake was the chief English Pirate & had a large Drum & sailed round the World in the Golden Hound (a ship). He did many other things like stealing Spanish treasure fleets & even, on one occasion a Spanish Mule train, which was also full of mules. He then singed the King of Spain's beard, which did little to improve international relations. Elizabeth was so pleased with all of this that she knighted him on the spot, & so he became Sir Francis. Drake was also good at playing boles, as will be seen later.

A SCOTCH PROBLEM

Meanwhile Elizabeth, like most English Kings & Queens, soon discovered that she had a Scotch problem, which was bound to happen sooner or later. This happened when Mary Queen of Scotch ran away from her Scotch subjects into England to ask her cousin Liz for Asylum. Liz replied: "I'll give you that alright," & locked her up in an English castle.

Mary was an R.C. & a Fame Fatale, as she had already been through 4 husbands, including the French Dolphin, & her Italian secretary. One of them, Lord Dunley was even blown up with gunpowder. Thus Mary did not trust men too much & changed all her Palace guard to women. Of course, most Scotch were Protestant & their leader John Noakes called Mary & her Palace guard "A Monstrous Regiment of Women"

& locked Mary up. But, as we have seen, she escaped to England & this gave Liz a headache, because Mary had a claim to the throne.

So Mary got involved with many plots like the Frog Morton plot & the Rudolpho plot against Glory Anna.

Here Liz drew the line ... on Mary's neck, & that was the end of Mary & the origin of the expression "To draw the line"!

THE SPANISH RAMADA

The Spanish had by now decided to invade England with a very large fleet, which being so large was not so much a fleet as a "Ramada". But there was a flaw in the Spanish plan, because while the Ramada was in Spain, the Spanish army was waiting for a lift in quite a different place, Carlisle, which is a pretty eccentric place for anyone to be at any time, let alone a whole Spanish army.

When the Ramada got within sight of Plymouth Ho, Drake was playing bowls with rubbers & said: "I'll finish those rubberneckers", as he had noticed that they were all sight-seeing at the time. This said, he bowled his last rubber of the game & set sail carrying his big Drum with him. He hurried & harried the Spanish right up the Chunnel, all the time beating his Drum which terrified the Duns who thought it was the sound of a very large gun, or even a Supercannon.

When the Ramada tried to anchor at Carlisle to pick up their soldiers, Drake sent in suicide fireships which terrified the Spanish even more, as they were full of double-shotted cannons & crewed by half-witted goons (who were expendable). In a panic they cut their anchor ropes & ran away backwards shouting "Hell burners!" as they thought Drake was the Devil & had a magic mirror. This is, of course, the origin of the expression "To sling your hook". Also the Spanish soldiers thus also missed their lift, which is the origin of the expression "To miss the boat". Drake's use of these Hell burners was probably against the Geneva Convention, being weapons of Mass Destruction, but was completely successful & therefore O.K.

Meanwhile, Sir Francis continued to hairy the Ramada all the way anti-clockwise round the entire British isles: England, Scotland & Ireland. All the time they had to sail backwards as they dared not take their eyes off Drake, & for this reason many of them were wrecked on the rocks & had to land in Ireland where they were massacred by I.R.A. wreckers, but were still the origin of the Black Irish.

While all this was going on the Virgin Queen was at Tilbury haranging & hanging her soldiers, telling them she had the heart & stomach of a King (not a Queen), & this unsurprisingly led to a lot of smutty laughter, hence the hanging.

So that was the end of the Spanish Ramada. A few years later the English had their own Ramada, but as this was unsuccessful, & in fact a complete disaster, it is not memorable, & we will waste no further time on it.

THE END OF THE TUDORS

Elizabeth I finished her reign by commissioning a set of wooden false teeth, & executing all her surviving suitors, which is the origin of the Expression "Off with their heads!", a famous line from the book "Alex in Wonderland". Thus the English had run completely out of Tudors, R.I.P.

THE WILLIAM SHAKESPEARE COMPANY

At sometime during Elizabeth's reign a new play & poetry wrighting company started up in Stortford on Avon. They were so good that they are remembered to this day in folios. For many years it was erroneously believed that there was just one William Shakespeare, but modern research has shown that there were several, maybe a dozen, Shakespeares each spelling their names slightly differently. Only one was not called Shakespeare - he was Francis Bacon. Altogether, at times it must have got pretty hectic in Ann Havaways cottage.

The famous works of this company are known the world over now with such immortal lines as:

"To be or not to be, that is the question." (Hamlit)

Or: "To buy - too steep! Perchance too dear." (also Hamlit)

Or: "Lay on me, MacDuff ect." (MacDeth)

Or: "Where the B. sucks, there sucks I." (Midsummer Nights Dram)

Or: "My Kingdom for a hearse!" (Richard III)

Or: "Romeo, Romeo, wherefore art thou Romeo?" (whatever that means) (Romeo & Juliet)

So you can see the William Shakespeares were pretty hot stuff.

Historical Aptitude & Intelligence Test
Test Paper 4: The Tudor Dinestry
(1 hour 30 mins)

1. Are VIII Queens better than I? Be specific.

2. How did Ann of Chives get converted from the Fair Maid of Flanders to the Fat Mare of Flanders? Could this be called a makeover?

3. What did Henry VIII mean exactly when he said, "Heads will roll"? Keep it brief.

4. Why were there so many Pretenders like Lambeth Simnel, Parking Wartback & Lady Zane Grey?

5. Was Edward VI largely unnecessary?

6. Why was the Stir Chamber useful to Henry VII?

7. Just how bloody was Mary? Be graphic.

8. With reference to the Spanish Ramada, what was the importance of the following: (a) Rubber bowls (b) Drake's drum (c) Fireships (d) Spanish gallons (e) Sailing backwards.

9. Is it possible that Queen Elizabeth I was actually a man? (Baring it in mind that Julia Caesar was probably a woman.)

10. Why could the Scotch problem never be properly solved?

11. What could possibly be the cause of the sinking of the Merry Rose other than a loose cannon? Was this a Good Thing? (& why?)

12. Describe the Renuissance (if possible).

13. Outline the story of **one** of the following: (a) MacDeth (b) Much a bore about nothing (c) A Midsummer Night's dram (d) Et tu Brute?

14. Why was Martin Luther confined to a Diet of Worms? Was this a breach of the Geneva Convention?

15. Spell Protestant.

THE END!

H.A.I.T. Test Paper 4:
Model Answer Specimen
(from a candidate in Donnegal)

1. Yes definitely, as long as heads can be rolled efficiently & without undue delay.

2. Because, although Henry VIII's IVth wife, he thought she was a harse & shipped her back to Flanders in a cattle truck with 7 other old cows.

3. Answered in 1.

4. This was because they all wanted a job in the Palace, & Lambert Simnel got it as a stallion. The others were less lucky.

5. Edward VII was too young & had to use Lord's Protectives & anyway he died of consummation in only 6 years.

6. The Stir Chamber helped Henry VII clear up any nobles left over from the Wars of the Roses by fining them for being livery & maintenance, & the putting them in stir to prevent complaints & compliance.

7. Incredibly so, with Carlisle written on her heart.

8. (a) A good story (b) Very important in frightening the Dons (c) Unfair to the Ramada which had to sling it's hook (d) Spanish gallons were much bigger than English gallons & so easier to hit with cannon balls or even rubber bowls (e) Very necessary when being chased by Drake

9. Well, she certainly admitted that she had the heart & stomach of a King.

10. Because Scotch are Scotch.

11. Probably speeding, trying to corner too fast, over the limit, top-heavy construction ... you name it.

12. Impossibly vague.

13. Can I do Hamlit please instead? Hamlit: Hamlit saw a ghost who turned out to be his father, the ex-King of Denmark murdered by his brother Claudius while asleep in the ear. Claudius had then seized the Crown & Hamlit's mother, making him a bl—dy, bl—dy villain. Hamlit decided that he must kill him, but only succeeded in stabbing Baloneyus behind the Arasse. This went on till the final scene when Hamlit poisoned his mother & stabbed Claudius with a poisoned sword, before dying himself of the same cause. So, in the last scene everyone was dead. (It must have been a good day for the Danish Royal Undertaker!)

(Examiner's note: It was decided to allow this answer because of its extreme accuracy.)

14. This was because he had burned a Papal Bull, declaring himself to be henceforth a vegetarian.

15. PROSTRATANT.

CHAPTER 5

THE STUARTS (OR STEWARTS)

E ngland had now run right out of Welsh Kings & Queens so it was decided to let the Scotch have a go. It was also thought that this might solve the Scotch problem once & for all. Some hope!

The first of these was called James VI of Scotland but he was a disagreeable man who was known to be the wisest fool in Christendom (if you can work out what *that* meant). Furthermore, James resented the English because:-

a. They had cut off his Mum's head (Mary q. of Scotch)

b. They had demoted him by taking away his VI, & reducing him to James I. This made him feel less than he had done before.

c. They had tried to blow him up in Parliament.

d. All other Scotch Jameses before him had been killed in battles with the English.

e. He was Scotch, very.

Since Elizabeth's reign there had arisen a lot of Puritans who were not proper C. of E. & wanted no bishops, & probably no Kings either. They also dressed invariably in black & were very strict when any morality was involved. Many of these had become M.P.s & James did not like that so he went into Parliament & told them that HE had Divine Light & so they could all shut up as **HE** was the boss, so there! He also told them to stop saying, "No bishop, No King." This did not go down at all well.

THE GUNPOWDER PLOT

While James I was thus haranguing Parliament, underneath it Guy Fawkes, a plotter, was busy loading the cellar with barrels & barrels of Gunpowder because he not only wanted No bishops & No Kings, but No M.P.s either! Guy, of course, being a plotter wore a long beard & a big black hat, as all good plotters should. The plan was to blow Parliament on firework night in the hope that the explosion might not be noticed with all the other bangs going off.

But at the last moment, poor Guy forgot his matches, so he was caught in the nick of time by the Beefeaters who thus prevented the King & Parliament from being blown to smithereens, not to mention the bishops! Hence the origin of the expression "Lost the Plot". Poor Guy was naturally hung, drawn & slaughtered.

All of this of course did not make the King any more secure, & he invariably wore a flak jacket & padded clothing in case anyone took a pop at him. Nevertheless he continued to say many wise things, although he had favourites, & this was unwise.

CHARLES I & THE ENGLISH CIVIL WAR

Charles I was a Cavalier King & always dressed very Cavalierly & spoke very Cavalierly to Parliament, especially about ship money (as he wanted to build a Navy). Like his father he also believed in Divine Light & told everyone so, including the Puritans in Parliament. But the Puritans continued to defy him & absolutely refused to give him any money at all.

Finally he decided to purge Parliament & marched troops in, making the excuse that some of his birds had flown. However Parliament refused to be abolished & this started the Civil War.

The Civil War had a good many battles most of which were fought at Newbury to be more easily remembered. At first the King did well as he had Prince Rupert, who invariably charged furiously on horseback & in all directions at once. Later however Parliament discovered that they had Oliver Cromwell, who developed a new army of tapsters & serving men called the New Motel Army (because they travelled a lot). He also invented many new types of soldiers like Ironsides, Iron Roundheads, Lobsters, ect. Thus eventually Parliament won.

Unfortunately, though Parliament had won the civil war, it had become just a RUMP, & an Addled one at that. So Oliver Cromwell said that Pride demanded that this Rump be Purged. He therefore marched his soldiers into Parliament & sent it back home, & this was called Pride's Purge. So Parliament & the King **both** lost the Civil war, & the only real winner was Oliver Cromwell himself who thus became the Lord Protective!

As for the Cavalier King Charles, he was locked up & began plotting (like his Granny, Mary Q. of Scotch). In fact his plots were so successful that he persuaded the Scotch, who were now called Conveners, to invade England twice. This infuriated Oliver as he had to keep defeating the Scotch which distracted him from the more important tasks of beating up the Rump, leftover Cavaliers, Addled Parliaments, Long Parliaments, Short Parliaments, Levellers, Diggers (early Australian immigrants), the Irish, & even the French. It is not certain that all this was a Good Thing.

So Charles I was put on trial for High Treeson, by Oliver & his Puritan cronies. The King continued to argue that He had the Divine Light to BE HEAD of the country, but the Puritans argued that they had the Divine Light to BEHEAD him, & then beheaded him to prove it!

So began a period without a King (or even a Queen) & just a Lord Protective. This period was known as the Commonwealth, though no-one really knows why.

Thus now Oliver was definitely Top Ruler & had his portrait done Warts 'n All. He also put the country under the rule of all his Sergeant-Majors who used Marshall Law & drilled everyone all over the place; an unpopular move.

By now the English had decided that they wanted a King again (or even a Queen) & so offered the Crown to Oliver, who rudely told them to, "Take away that Buboe," & dismissed them abruptly.

So when Cromwell died, it was decided to bring back the Stuarts (which may or may not have been A Good Thing). This was called the Reformation.

THE REFORMATION OF CHARLES II, THE MERRY MONARCH

Charles II was not only Merry, he was also very Romantic as he had spent a good deal of his early life successfully hiding from Roundheads, mainly in hollow oak trees in Sherwood forest. He was also very handsome with long curly well-permed hair & a Clark Gable moustache. So he was very popular with all the ladies except his wife, Queen Catherine of Briganda (in Portugal), & had many mistresses including Nell Gwyn, the famous inventor of Marmalade.

Unfortunately having all these mistresses led to a large influx of Royal Bastards, Old, Young & Middle-aged Pretenders, Dukes, Earls, ect.

The new King told his friends that he wanted to die with his boots OFF, unlike his father, so he decided to treat Parliament nicely & not mention things like Divine Light or Ship Money, ect. This was wise because there were still plenty of Puritans around, & even some Roundheads.

Unfortunately disasters struck Charles II. The first of these was the great plague of London, followed immediately by the Great Fire of London. The Fire began when someone lost control of a Pudding that they were cooking in a Lane, which burned down half of London. The King himself helped the firefighters, but in those days fires were stopped by pulling down the houses with a hook, so the half of London not burned down was pulled down. Luckily a great architrave called Sir Christopher Robin rebuilt St. Paul's Cathedral & most of the rest of London.

Because the King did not dare to ask Parliament for Ship money, a Dutch Admiral tied a broom to his mast & swept up the Thames, towing away the entire Royal Navy.

In spite of all these disasters, Charles continued to be Reformed, Merry & a Monarch & died with his boots off as he had wanted.

JAMES II

With Charles II having died correctly with his boots off (unlike his father Charles I who had died incorrectly with his boots on but his head off) the next Stuart King was James II. Unfortunately, contrary to the country James was R.C. not C. of E., & stubbornly so. This worried the C. of E. English because James wanted to make all M.P.s, Army officers, Professors, future Kings & even bishops R.C. instead of C. of E. This led to a Rebellion by a Royal Bastard Duke called Moanmouth who raised a Pheasant army in the South West, claiming that he was not really a Bastard, was C. of E., & should therefore be King. But poor Moanmouth was defeated by the Regular Army under Marlboro, who now all correctly wore red coats. This battle at Sludgemoor was the last battle to be fought on English soil (but not Scotch of course). Moanmouth's pheasants only had primitive weapons like sickles & scythes (see earlier under "The Ancient Brits") & were therefore easily defeated by the Regulars. Moreover, when they tried to run away their feet became firmly stuck in the sludge of Sludgemoor, so they were slaughtered to a man.

THE BLOODY DOWNSIZES

Moanmouth was quickly downsized (or shortened) by having his head cut off, as was the custom those days. Judge Jeffries then toured the South West downsizing many of the pheasants who had supported Moanmouth in a memorably brutal manner, & "preferably with a blunt axe". It is now considered doubtful if this was a Good Thing.

Meanwhile, the Queen, who had previously been barren, gave birth to a male heir in a warming pan. This was a new (probably French) method of giving birth, but did not please the English, especially as it was probably French. So it was decided to have a Glorious Revolution.

THE GLORIOUS REVOLUTION

The English were now fed up with James II after only 3 years because of his R.C.ism & decided that it was time for a new set of Monarchs. They decided they must stick to the rule that no Monarch could be English, & so they chose a Dutchman, William of Orange, who had a female Stuart wife, Mary. So William invaded successfully because of Protestant wind (a nasty complaint, especially for by-standers). And James left the country without bloodshed & so the Glorious Revolution wasn't really a Revolution at all, being completely bloodless[9], but was certainly Glorious. This was definitely a Good Thing.

The only drawback to all this was that it gave rise to a fresh outbreak of Pretenders - there were Old Pretenders, Young Pretenders & naturally Middle-aged Pretenders also. This Pretender outbreak lasted a long time - over 50 years, & caused yet another Scotch problem, & even an Irish one too[10]. The supporters of these new Pretenders were all called Jacobines, though it is not now known why.

---

[9] Some years later the French taught the English the correct procedure for doing Revolutions which must be extremely bloody, by having the memorable French Revolution.

[10] This also gave rise to a serious outbreak of Orange men who wore orange sashes & bowler hats, & all lived in Lodges like beavers, & paraded around a lot. Some of them even had gons too!

As William was only a Dutchman & only really an apprentice King, never having been one before, it was thought that he would need watching. So his Stuart wife Mary was appointed equal Monarch & would do this job. Thus he was known as "William 'n Mary" instead of "Just William". It was also ruled that henceforth all MALE Stuarts were Pretenders, whereas all FEMALE Stuarts (e.g. Mary & Ann) were O.K. & could be Monarchs. A clear early victory for 17th century Feminists.

William of Orange was chiefly concerned with fighting wars against the powerful French King Louis XIV, also called "Le Roi Soleil" or the "Sunburned King". But he also spent a lot of time beating up Jacobines, especially in Ireland (The Battle of the Boyen). He also approved of a massacre of Scotch MacDonald Jacobines at Glascoe (or Glengow) which was probably NOT a Good Thing, although it kept the Scotch problem on ice for some time.

Finally, out riding one day, William 'n Mary's horse tripped over a small gentleman in black velvet, & the former died of his injuries.

QUEEN ANNE

The two most important historical facts about Queen Anne were that (a) she utterly failed to have any more Stuarts & so became the last, & (b) she was dead anyway! This meant that the English had now used up all the Stuarts (except the Jacobine Pretenders of course, but they didn't count).

But nevertheless during her very short reign the memorable Marlboro kept up the fight against the French Louis 14, the "Sunburned King". This resulted in four extremely memorable English victories at Odournade, Rommelies, Blenham & Malfunction. This was, of course, a Good Thing & gave rise to Blenham Palace[11] & eventually also to Winston Churchill (as Marlboro's real surname was Churchill) - another Very Good Thing. This war was called "The Spanish Succession", though no-one now knows why.

Thus finally ended the Stuart dinnersty & so a new set of non-English Monarchs was needed. It was decided that since the Germans had not yet had a go, it was only fair to give them a chance. These Germans were the rulers of a small German state called Hunnover & were therefore Huns. Although rulers they were not so much actual "Kings" as "Selectors", because Hunnover was too small to be an actual "Kingdom". Thus, like William 'n Mary they had no experience as Kings & so would need watching, especially as they couldn't even **speak** English! Previously, if a King (or even a Queen) had needed watching it had been done by a "Lord Protective", but as this hadn't worked too well the English invented a new solution (see next chapter). As a general rule these new Hunnoverian Kings were all called "George" (see also next chapter).

---

[11] Blenham Palace can still be seen today (at a price!).

Historical Aptitude & Intelligence Test
Test Paper 5: The Stuarts
(1 hour 30 mins)

Candidates should attempt ALL questions which they regard as being reasonable!

1. How did Guy Fowks lose the plot? Was this A Good Thing?

2. Explain the meaning & importance of the following memorable expressions: (a) No bishop, no King (b) The wisest fool in Christendom (c) Divine Light (d) The birds have flown.

3. Should Puritans have been allowed - especially in Parliament? Give your reasoning (if any).

4. Was Oliver Cromwell a breach of the Geneva Convention?

5. Should Charles I have been allowed to BE HEAD, or should he have been BEHEADED? Keep it short.

6. Explain the importance of each of the following: (a) The Rump (b) Lord Protectives (c) Buboes (d) Ironsides.

7. Outline the achievements of Sir Christopher Robin. But should London have been rebuilt after the Great Fire anyway?

8. In what ways did the infamous Judge Jeffries downsize Moonmouth's pheasants?

9. What was the significance of (a) Old Pretenders (b) Young Pretenders (c) New Pretenders & Middle-Aged Pretenders?

10. Why was William 'n Mary not Just William?

11. Explain how Queen Anne was the real cause of the Hunnovers.

12. How did Marlboro deal with the French Sunburned King?

THE END!

H.A.I.T. Test Paper 5:
Model Answer Specimen

1. Guy Forks failed by getting caught with his matches down & thus also getting hung, drawn & slaughtered.

2. (a) No bishop, No King was what the Roundheads said before they abolished bishops, & even Kings (b) A French saying, & therefore meaningless (c) Divine Light was something Kings had, but Parliament didn't (except Oliver Cromwell) (d) A coded message sent by carrier pigeon.

3. No, Puritans shouldn't have been allowed because they led to Roundheads & Oliver Cromwell, warts 'n all.

4. Definitely, because he abolished Charles I.

5. It depends on your point of view, but I personally am opposed to corporal punishment.

6. (a) The Rump: so-called because it was the backside of Parliament (b) Protectives are necessary when you run out of Kings (or even Queens) (c) Not easy to explain (d) Ironsides were necessary if you wanted to defeat Prince Rudolph's cavalier calvary.

7. Sir Christopher Robin, a brilliant architrave, rebuilt the whole of London in a completely different style which was A Good Thing.

8. Judge Jeffries downsized Moonmouth's revolting pheasants by reducing their height by a head.

9. This is a Good Question ... (in other words I don't have a clue) sorry.

10. William 'n Mary could not be Just William because he was a Dutch Orange, & anyway only an apprentice King

as he had had no experience in the job, & thus needed watching.

11. Because Queen Anne was invariably dead.

12. Marlboro beat the French & their Sunburned King at Spanish Succession.

CHAPTER 6
THE HUNNOVERIANS &
THE BUILDING OF THE EMPIRE

As the last Stuart Queen Anne was now invariably dead, a new set of German Kings from Hunnover had to be introduced, & this started the 18th century. As a general rule these Hunnoverian Kings were invariably called George (either I, II, III, or IV). They lasted all the way to Queen Victoria who broke the sequence by marrying a German consul called Prince Albert, & thereby converted the Royal family into Sack-Coalbags, & built the Albert Hall to prove it.

The new German Kings could not speak English so it was thought necessary to invent a Prime Minister to keep them in order. Another new invention was political parties called Whigs & Tories, though no-one knew the difference. Whether these innovations were a Good Thing is debatable.

The first P.M. in recorded history was called Sir Robert Walpole who devised the excellent policy of doing nothing at all & letting sleeping dogs lie.

THE SOUTHSEA BUBBLE

About this time an enormous Bubble was discovered at Southsea. Incredibly the existence of this Bubble led to the formation of a huge number of equally incredible new Companies in which many foolish people invested all their life savings. Inevitably after getting bigger & bigger the Bubble suddenly burst, & all these new investors were ruined. In spite of this P.M. Walpole stuck to his policy of doing nothing at all, which was probably very wise!

YET ANOTHER SCOTCH PROBLEM: "THE 45"

In spite of the Hunnoverians there were still Jacobines around, especially in the wild Helands of Scotland, so a Young Pretender left over from the Stuarts called Bonnie[12] Prince Charlie took advantage of this & arrived in the Helands from France with 45 followers. Of course this was altogether wrong, but extremely wromantic. The Prince then gathered as many of the Clans as he could & invaded England with bands of wild Helanders, all wearing tartan skirts & making hideous bag noises (see earlier references to Scotch problems). These Helanders won many romantic battles against the redcoats, except the last one, which solved the problem.

Nevertheless the Bonnie Prince managed to escape & had many romantic adventures in the wild Helands with his girlfriend Flora MacDonald before cleverly escaping back to France in a Bonnie boat. If you want to know more about all

---

[12] It is not definitely known why he was called "Bonnie", but some believe he may have been mistaken for a girl as he often wore a tartan skirt & dress & had a pretty face & hair (a sine qua non if you want to be Romantic).

this read Sir Walter Scot, who was also Scotch but very Romantic.

This was luckily the very last Scotch problem in History, as the Scotch finally agreed to be British, as long as they could keep their Tartan Army!

THE FOUNDING OF THE BRITISH EMPIRE

As by this time the Spanish, Portuguese, Dutch & even French had Empires, it was thought that the British should also have one, & most importantly it should be the **BIGGEST!**

A century before Sir Walter Rally had got the ball rolling (so to speak) by discovering that North America had tobacco & potatoes, & so he brought them back to England. So the U.S.A. became the first British colony (at least until it was discovered that Americans were mean & greedy & refused to pay taxes, didn't like tea & even refused to do their duty & buy Stamps! (See later under "The American War of Dependents".)

Anyway, as the XVIIIth century had now arrived the British got serious about the Empire State building. This was mainly done by an outbreak of new Prime Ministers who were invariably called Pitt. There were Older Pitts, Young Pitts & Pitts the Younger, to mention but a few.

These Pitt P.M.s cunningly joined all the wars going in the 18th century (& there were many of these), in order to keep all the other European countries occupied, especially the French, so that none of them would notice that the British were quietly making their Empire. These wars were invariably called Wars of Succession, & were always against the French. Thus Marlboro began the 18th century correctly by causing the War of Spanish Succession, & this was followed by the War of Austrian Succession, then Russian, then Prussian, then Italian, then Dutch, ect., ect. However the Pitts always cleverly avoided having a War of English Suc-cession.

It should be explained that these Wars of Succession were fought to decide how Successful each King (or Emperor & Queen) had been in Succeeding to his (or her) throne, & more importantly, how Successful he (or she) had been in staying put on it.

But when the British ran out of Succession Wars, they craftily invented new wars like the War of Jenkin's Ear, the War of Hobson's Choice, & the 7 Year's War. The last one was so called because no-one could think of anything less boring to call it, & when things quietened down too much, the British pulled other stunts to keep the others distracted. On one of these occasions they even shot one of their own Top men, Admiral Binge, on his own deck. This was bitterly criticised by the imminent French Philosopher Vulture, but he was only jealous, & anyway he was French!

While all this hullaballoon was going on, no-one noticed that elsewhere the British were quietly filching their Empire, by stealth attacks, mainly of course from the French. Thus, for instance, General Wolf took Quebec by using Muffled oars, & so Canada became a British colony. Likewise General Clive craftily escaped from a Black Hole in Calcutta & defeated the French, thus taking India. The British then wisely converted the Eastern part of India into a Company called John Company. Similarly the West Indies were en-filaded, & their rich punters began to grow sugar, malaises & of course Rum. Many other colonies & islands were amalgamated & so, at last, the British Empire was the **biggest** in the entire world, & all the Atlases had to be coloured red.

What the Red Indians & Indian Indians thought of all this is unknown & was therefore thought to be unimportant. But it was jolly good news for many English colonellists who wanted to become Rubber Punters, Pucker Sarbs, Guvnor Generals or Vinceroys & play the great game called chota pegging, & go pig-stinking or tiger hunting with tiffin guns (even though the heat *could* send you to Doolally).

SLAVERY: A REGRETTABLE FACT & VERY BAD THING

Slavery & its trade were a regrettable fact of the Empire & completely **Politically Incorrect & against the Geneva Convention & the U.N. (& even NATO)** until it was abolished by the great British Filanthropist William Wilderfarce. The first Brit to incorrectly profit from the Slave trade had been Sir John Hawking back in the days of Glory Anna. It was all caused by the fact that the rich punters in the West Indies wanted slaves to make sugar & Rum, & those in the Southern states of America wanted them to make cotton & Gin. Luckily, in the end this was all abolished which was a Very Good Thing.

GEORGE III, THE MAD KING

George III was the first of the Georges to actually speak English, but he had one disadvantage: he was utterly bonkers. This was noticed when he began to shake hands with all the trees in Winser park, even greeting one of them as the King of Prussia, & other Kings, Emperors, ect. He often thought he was a dog (hence the expression "barking mad") or Napoleon Bornapart, & he addressed Parliament as "My Lords & Peecox". Thus his son had to be appointed

Prince Regnant, as Lord Protectives were now thoroughly out of date. The Prince Reganant was a very dissolute man, with disreputable friends like Bow Bummel. As he did very little but drink brandy, build pavilions in Brighton & try to Polygonously marry one Mrs. FitzHumbartz, it was just as well that there were still some of the memorable outbreak of Pitts left over to run the country properly.

THE AMERICAN WAR OF DEPENDENTS

Meanwhile in the American colonys the colonelists were getting restless & refusing to pay taxes or buy stamps or even to do their Duty by drinking Tea! They made up the slogan "No taxation without Presentation" because they were angry at not being presented to the British Parliament. Finally they all met together dressed as Indians at a fancy dress party in the harbour at Boston to show that they really only liked coffee by throwing all the tea into the water. This was of course clearly revolting.

One of the leaders of the American rabbles was the clever Benjamin Shanklin who had invented electricity by flying a kite in a lightning storm. Another was George Washington who was unique because he never told a lie, did not cut down a pear tree, & even had wooden teeth! But the most important was Jefferson Davis, a brainy man who lived in a famous house called Monty Cello. He was a clever writer who wrote the Declaration of Dependents which declared that all American colonelists were Dependents but wanted to be Independents. This all started the American war of Dependents which was the first & only war that the British actually lost.

The first battle was the Battle of Bunkum hill, although it was actually fought on a different hill. It was quickly discovered that typically the revolting American colonelists did not fight fair, hiding behind trees & rocks without proper uniforms & shooting at the neat, straight lines of British redcoats. This dastardly breach of the Geneva convention rules[13] of war was, unfortunately, successful. They also persuaded an Indian tribe called the Morricans to fight on their side to the last man, who was called "The Last of the Morricans". He had a wife called Minny. (Ha ha!)

Typically once the war had started, the dastardly French joined the revolting Americans, as they saw that here was a chance to actually win a war against the British. Moreover other unfriendly countries like Russia pretended to like the Americans & blockaded British trade by the "Armed Neuterality". Of course this was all completely unfair, but unfortunately also memorable. Thus overall the British lost which was a thoroughly Bad Thing.

Meanwhile Jefferson Davis, encouraged by the success of his publication of the Declaration of Dependents, invented & wrote an entirely New Thing called The Constitutional. This stated that henceforth all Americans (except slaves of course)[14] had the Right to "Life, to take Liberties & the pur-

---

[13] The rules for 18th century wars made it quite clear that battles must be fought in **straight lines** by soldiers in **identical brightly-coloured uniforms,** & wear powdered Whigs, ect. E.g. the British always wore red uniforms, the French blue & the Austrians white. This made them easier to see on the battlefield (and shoot also). Moreover an officers' meeting must be held before each battle to decide which side got the privilege of firing the first volley. Thus the American method of fighting was very clearly unfair.

[14] Jefferson Davis owned his own slaves, but being a taking liberty lover actually thought that slavery was a Bad Thing, & would later be what he called "A Fireball in the Night".

suit of Happiness", which they have done ever since, as we all know to our cost!

Jefferson's Constitutional also invented a new kind of Parliament called Congress, & stated that all future American Kings would be elected every so often & would not be called "Kings" but "Presidents", & could take more liberties. Furthermore the Constitutional had at the end a long list of Commandments which could not in any way be mended (i.e. changed) unless absolutely everyone agreed, & so, as this is clearly impossible, even 200 years later none of these Commandments has **ever** been changed, & Americans still carry guns.

Thus the British finally lost the American colonys, & the colonelists said that it was "Manifest Chastity", invented a new flag called "The Star Swindled banner", bought New Olleans & Lousyanna off the French & became foreign for good. They even refused to speak English properly to prove that they were now truly Independents.

Naturally all this made George III even madder, but luckily, just in time the memorable explorer & navicater Captain Cook replaced the loss by discovering Australia & New Zealand.

THE FRENCH REVOLUTION

Having helped the Revolting American colonelists, the French now decided to round off the 18th century by having a Revolution of their own. Furthermore, they wanted to show other nations how to have a **proper** Revolution which was **thoroughly Revolting.**

The whole thing was planned by a club called the Jacobines who lived in a Tennis court & took a lot of Oaths. They decided that as "proper Revolutionaries" they must:-

1. Abolish all Kings called Louis. This was hardly surprising as they were currently on their XVIth Louis!

2. Abolish the Queen, Mary Antonette because she wanted to put the Paris Yobs on bread & water, & anyway she was a foreigner from Australia.

3. Abolish the Dolphins so that there couldn't be any more Kings called Louis (or anything else, come to that!).

4. Abolish the Astrocrats (Ducs, Conts, ect.) who all lived in luxury in their shateaus & treated their pheasants abominably.

5. Abolish the priests because, as R.C.s, they didn't want to make any more awkward confessions.

6. Abolish all foreigners as they were not French Patriots.

7. Abolish a rival group of Revolutionaries called the "Gerundives" (because they all lived next to a river called the Gerund, near the provincial city of Bordow).

In this Revolution the Jacobines were greatly helped by a new invention which made their task much easier. This was invented by a French barber called Dr. Gillette (who was distantly related to Sweeney Todd), & was therefore called the "Gilletine" or "National Razor" (or Erazor). This machine was a labour saving device for removing heads, or indeed any other inconvenient parts of the body more cleanly & efficiently.

The main Jacobines who led the new Revolution were, in order of atrocity: Roguespear, nicknamed "The Pea green Incorruptible", Dante (who was in contrast very Corruptible & got Gilletined for it), Murat, who got stabbed in his bath by an angry Gerundive - see later, St. Jest, nicknamed the "Angle of Death", Merrybore (who incorrectly didn't want to

Gilletine the Royals, & so got Gilletined himself!), & Lafagette (who had helped the American revolters).

Before getting their Revolution under way, the Jacobines made up a new slogan: "Libertine, Eggality, Friternity" (which fortunately no-one actually understood) & invented a new flag called the Tricorner. They also invented a new Patriotic song, which is **still** the French Natural Anthem: "Allons Infants de la Pastrie / La jour de Gloire ay arrivée" ect.

Having made all these careful preparations, the Jacobines raised the Paris Yobs, who lived in Forburgs (French for "Paris slums"). These Yobs all wore red Friesian caps to symbolise Liberty, & wore absolutely no trousers (to symbolise Taking Liberties), & so were called "Sankalots" (French for "No britches").

The Paris Yobs started the Revolution by storming a big prison called the Bustille, letting out all the prisoners & erasing the building to the ground. They then attacked the Twilleries Palace & massacred all the Swish[15] guards. The King, Queen, Dolphins & Princesses were then all abolished with the Gilletine, which made poor George III across the Chunnel even madder. & all the other Kings, Emperors, Queens, ect. in all the other countries worry that they too might get Abolished by their own Yobs!

Soon too the Astrocrats were Gilletined by the score. They were taken to the Gilletine in tumblers, which must have been uncomfortable in itself, never mind having your head erazed! A few of these Astrocrats escaped by Immigration ("Immigrés") & some were saved by a mysterious Scarlet Pimpel in disguise, according to a writer called Alexander Dumass.

---

[15] They were called this because of their smart red uniforms.

The Revolution soon spread to the country areas where the abominably treated pheasants attacked the Shateaus & killed their own Astrocrats. This part of the Revolution was called a "Jackerie" because French pheasants were invariably called Jack.

The next to get Gilletined by the Jacobines were a rival Revolutionary club called the Gerundives. But one of them, a young Madamoselle called Charlotte Cordy got back by stabbing Murat *in* the bath, though what she was doing in his bath has never been explained (but, being French ...).

This was all, of course, a very Bad Thing, but luckily, having run out of Kings, Queens, Dolphins, Princesses, Astrocrats, Gerundives & foreigners to abolish, the Jacobines got bored with having no-one to Gilletine, & began to abolish each other! This was caused by a new Committee formed by Roguespear & his friend St. Jest (The Angle of Death). It was called the Committee of "Public Safety", & made *it* pretty unsafe to be French, even if you were also revolting!

THE END OF THE FRENCH REVOLUTION

Meanwhile the French Chief of Police was getting very fed up with all this Revolutionary Badlam & Hullaballoon. However, he cunningly waited until Roguespear & St. Jest had Gilletined **all** the other Jacobines, & then arrested the two last Jacobines & abolished them before they knew what was happening! Finally a new young Army officer called Napoleon Bornapart added the finishing touchpaper by bringing his canons into the streets of Paris & blowing away the last remaining revolting Sankalots with a "Whiff of Crapshot".

Thus ended the French Revolution to the great relief of all. Everything had been abolished by now, including Kings, Queens, Dolphins, Astrocrats, Priests, foreigners, Sankalots, Autocrats, Borbons, Gerundives & even Jacobines - the lot, in fact. So, as no-one was left, Napoleon Bornapart made France a Consulate (& then an Empire with **Himself** as Emperor, naturellement!).

Historical Aptitude & Intelligence Test
Test Paper 6: The 18th Century
(1 hour 30 mins)

1. Why did the English select the Hunnoverians to be the next set of Kings of England? Was it a wise choice? Give reasons, if any.

2. What was Sir Robert Walpole's policy? Was it wise?

3. Why did Bonnie Prince Charlie escape into the heather with Flora MacDonald? Keep it clean!

4. Why did the British Empire have to be the **BIGGEST**?

5. Discuss the importance of: (a) Pitts (b) Sir Walter Rawley (c) General Wolf (d) Admiral Binge.

6. Why were all the Wars of Succession necessary?

7. Outline the importance of each of the following: (a) Sugar Punters (b) Pucker Sarbs (c) Chota pegging (c) Pig stinking.

8. Why was a Prince Reganant needed for George **III**?

9. Why did the Revolting American colonelists not fight fair?

10. Discuss the advantages & disadvantages of Jefferson Davis's Constitutional.

11. What exactly **was** the Southsea Bubble? Was it a National phenomenon?

12. How did Captain Cook make George III less mad?

13. Was the French Revolution either: (a) Slightly Revolting (b) Fairly Revolting (c) Very Revolting or (d) Extremely Revolting? Give reasons for your answer if you can think of any.

14. Outline the nasty habits of the French Yobs & Sankalots.

15. What did the French Revolutionary Jacobines abolish, before abolishing themselves?

16. What exactly does "Libertine, Eggality & Friternity" actually mean? Be exact.

17. Why were the French Astrocrats a dying breed?

18. Write brief notes on each of the following: (a) The pea-green Incorruptible (Roguespear) (b) The Angle of Death (c) Louis XVI (d) Mary Antonette.

THE END!

H.A.I.T. Test Paper 6:
Model Answer Specimen
(for the benefit of future candidates)

1. Because Saxons, Normans, French, Welsh, Scotch & Dutch had all had a go at being Kings & Queens, & it was thought it was time that the Germans had a go, because England was politically correct & Multicultural. It was not a wise choice though because the Hunnoverians were all called George, & the first II could not even speak English[16], the IIIrd was raving bonkers, & the IV was a Prince Reganant, extremely dissolute & built hideous Pavilions, especially at Brighton (which can still be seen today, but shouldn't be!).

2. Sir Robert Walpole's policy was to completely & utterly ignore the phenomenal Southsea Bubble. This was very wise as it saved a fortune towards the Bank of England, which had just invented the National Debt (an extremely important new invention). Walpole countered this by inventing a sinking fund, which sank the Southsea Bubble before it was too late. He was also a dog lover & invariably let sleeping dogs lie.

3. Use your imagination!

4. The British Empire **had** to be the **BIGGEST** because the Spanish, French & Dutch Empires ect. were always unkind to their natives, so the British saved many natives from cruelty.

5. (a) Pitts came in all ages & invented the British Empire. (b) Sir Walter Rawley discovered Potatoes & Tobacco in the

---

[16] E.g. George I told the English that he had come for their own good, when he really meant that he had come for their own **goods**!

U.S. & brought them back to England. Without him Fish & Chips could never have been invented. (c) Gen. Wolf sneaked up on the French in Quebec & took Canada by naked stealth. (d) Admiral Binge was shot by his own side to encourage the other British Admirals to be more Admirable in the future! (According to the French philosopher Vulture, though what **He** knew about it is anyone's guess, cheeky Frog!)

6. All those "Wars of Succession" were to see how successful all the European Kings, Emperors, Queens, ect. could be at staying on their thrones.

7. (a) Sugar punters were important because they punted sugar in the West Indies & made Rum, without which the Royal Navy could **never** have won all the battles they did! (b) All British Sahibs in India had to be Pucker to prove to the natives that they were Top Nation & keep down Mutilations. (c) Chota pegging was an obscure & now-forgotten colonial game that involved pegging Chotas. (d) Pig stinking was another obscure Indian game, thankfully no longer practised!

8. The Prince Regenant was necessary because Lord Protectives were old-fashioned, & George III was barking mad & did strange things to trees.

9. The American rabbles broke the rules of Battle by **not** standing in straight lines in brightly-coloured uniforms. Instead they shot from behind trees, walls, rocks, ect. & did not give the redcoats a fair chance of shooting them back (typical Yank!).

10. Jefferson Davies's new U.S. Constitutional changed their Kings into "Presidents" & their Parliament into "Congresses" (just to be different!). It also had a lot of Com-mand-

ments which forced all U.S. citizens to carry guns at all times, because this was the Right to bare Arms. Unfortunately, they still have bare arms right up to the present day, including Charlton Heston.

11. The Southsea Bubble was an amazing phenomenon, but it must have existed or it wouldn't be in History, & be Memorable.

12. Captain Cook made George III less mad by replacing the lost American colonies with 2 brand new ones - Australia & New Zealand.

13. The French Revolution was extremely revolting because the Sankalots (Paris Rabbles) were not only revolting but also French. They didn't **even** have the decency to wear trousers!

14. The Sankalots (Paris Yob) took Liberties by abolishing all the Astrocrats & mass a kring all the Swish guards. They even drew a line on the King's neck.

15. The French Jacobines abolished practically everybody (including themselves), with the soul exception of Napoleon Bornapart.

16. The meaning of "Libertine, Eggality & Friternity" is anyone's guess, but nevertheless it is Memorable.

17. The French Astrocrats were a dying breed because they all got abolished, or Immigrated with the help of a Scarlet Pimpel.

18. (a) The Pea Green Incorruptible was so-called because he suffered from perannual indigestion so that his skin had a bilious greenish hew, & he also invariably wore green sunglasses. He was Incorruptible so that he could Gilletine all the Corruptibles, which included all the other

Jacobines, which he did. Unfortunately for him, the French chief of police was also Corruptible, & gilletined him back! (b) The Angle of Death, St. Jest, was Roguespear's closet friend (until he too got abolished). (c) Louis XVI - The French were fed up with Louis's after having XVI of them, & decided to draw the line at XVI. They also drew a line on his neck! (d) Mary Antonette, the Queen, had invested heavily in the Cake industry, & so also had to be abolished.

CHAPTER 7

THE INDUSTRIAL REVELATION & NAPOLEONIC WARS

THE INDUSTRIAL REVELATION

It all started in the Renuissance because Science was invented then, & this led to Inventions. For example the Italian Leonardo der Vinchy began by inventing the first heli-copters & tanks, ect., & drawing byological pictures of men, women (& even babies) cut in half to show the working parts, ect.

Meanwhile, another Italian, called Galley Leo had in-vented Astronamy by making the very first telescope, & thus discovered Moons on Jupiter & that there were canals on Mars, which has now been proved by the Nasser Apolo Missions. Another Astronamer called CopperNickelus found that the Moon goes round the Earth, or was it vicer-verser?

However **Real Science** was invented in England (naturally) by Sir Isaac Norton, who discovered that Apples invariably fell **Downwards & never Upwards.** He called this important new discovery Gravity, & to make sure it could never be changed he also cleverly made it into a **Law.** Being a modest man, he explained that he could not have done this without standing on the shoulders of a bunch of other scientists (to observe the Apples more closely). This was all very important because it started Physicks & Physickal Education, & many new Laws were made (e.g. Boil's Law, Murphy's Law, ect.) which was a Very Good Thing.

After all this, during the XVIIIth century, Chemistry was invented by the Alchemists (so-called because they were **All** Chemists). They proved by turning Bass metal into Gold thus starting the Pharmacutical Industry although this clever trick is now unfortunately lost!

Soon many new inventions were being made & this led to Machines & Mess-production. Arkwright invented the Spinning Jenny (with the help of his wife Jenny), & not content with this went on to make the Flying Shuttle (not to be confused with the Nasser astronuts Flying Space Shuttle, which came much later of course). These machines made cotton, although the rare material had to be imported from the cotton Punters in South America (who also made cotton gin & liked Mint Jollops, as they were a boozy lot!).

All these things took place in the North of England & caused a new class: the Working Class who all worked very, very hard for very, very, very little pay. It was also discovered that women, & even quite small children[17] could also work in factories & mines, ect., which was useful as it increased prophets no end, & made bags of Brass naturally. It also kept Parliament busy for over 100 years making new Acts - Factory Acts, Mine Acts & the like, which had to be a Good Thing as it kept M.P.s from corrupting & other misbehaviour!

---

[17] Schools had not yet been invented.

Of course all this meant that the North was soon covered in factories, mines & Dark Satanic Mills. A top poet called William Bleak wrote poetry about these Dark Satanic Mills - which is why the North was named "The Bleak country". He also wrote about Bows of Burning Gold (perhaps he was also a secret All Chemist) & Burning Arrows of Desire, though no-one knows why. All this was a Good Thing (unless you were Working class) & led to England being "The Sweatshop of the World". It also led to much muck & brass, & Mess-production. The only drawback was that the Mess-production caused an Environment, & so gave rise to Environ Mentalists.

STEAM POWER

This was discovered by a Scotchman called James What (?) who did it by simply boiling an egg, & this was important to drive all the new machines & make more Mess-production. Using this method, another Scotchman, Robert Lewis Stevenson built the first Railway[18] & even invented a Steam Rocket. With his engines it was possible to pull all the water out of the mines, which was necessary as coal was needed to drive the Steam engines! This was socially important as it caused British Rail, & meant everyone could go to the seaside, & so Holidays were invented - A Very Good Thing.

Thus the invention of steam led to many new machines & engines. There were steam railways & locamotives (a posh word for trains), steam ships, steam pumps, steam spinning jennies, steam baths, steam flying shuttles (which actually didn't fly), steam cars, steam lorries, steam tractors, steam

---

[18] The 1st. railway was built from Manchester to Blackpool as Stevenson did like to be beside the seaside, & he won fame by running over a Cabinet Minister called "Husky Son" on his very first trip!

trazction engines, steam submarines & even steam Rockets! Many of these machines ect. were deported all over the World, especially the Empire. For example steam trains were deported all the way to India, which led to Indian Railways, which still use them right up to this day! All this led to a huge outbreak of engineers.

All these new-fangled machines didn't please everyone, particularly the weevels who started a new organisation called the Lyddites. These Lyddites broke up many of these machines, & if they could not break them, they blew them up using a newly-invented gunpowder called Lyddite (hence the name). However, the Lyddites were eventually abolished because they were Revelationary, & Revelations were totally Illegal in England at the time. However a few of these Lyddites survived & were determined to keep on being Revelationary, & so took up conspiracies instead. One of these, called the Cato street conspiracy conspired to blow up the entire Cabinet (à la Gye Forks), which was a Very Bad Thing. Luckily however, they themselves were broken up before they could do this by Bow street Runners, who were actually policemen dressed up as Athletes!

The cleverest & most famous of **all** the new engineers was Islambard Kingdom Brownell who built the Great Western Railway himself, single-handed, thus allowing anyone who did not have a steam carriage to go on holiday in Cornwall, which is a long way. He also built the Chunnel right under the Thames which is now called the Black Hell Chunnel. He then went on to bridges made of iron, which was unusual because they were all made of iron, which had never been used before. A good example of this is the Cliveden suspension bridge at Brixton. But, after a while, he got fed up with Railways, Chunnels & Bridges, so he went on to ships. Brownell's ships were always very big, & this is why they were all called "The Great" something. To prove that they were all Great, Brownell always launched them **sideways**, which was unusual, in fact unique, but has never been tried since. One of them, "The Great Eastern" was so big, that some of the shipbuilders got lost in it, & were not found until many years later! Sadly, Brownell died after lighting his cigar too near one of his boilers, with unfortunate consequences.

Thus the Industrial Revolution was a Very Good Thing, because it made England "The Sweatshop of the World" & all Englishmen rich, except the Working Class of course, who had to remain very poor & overworked so that everyone else could be rich. It was also good because it made all the foreigners jealous, particularly the French, who also tried to build steam engines, & steam Rockets, but could only come up with a hot-air balloon, which was useless because you couldn't even steer it!

THE NAPOLEONIC WARS

Napoleon Bornapart was born apart from France on an island called Coarsica, but became an emigrant and thus French, though he always talked with a coarse Coarsican accent. He became an army officer, & as we have seen, abolished the entire French Revolution himself single-handed. As for any Revelationaries left over from the Revelation (there weren't many!) Bornapart easily abolished them too with a single "Whiff of Crapshot", making France into a Consolate (with **himself** as Chief Console, naturally). He then gained even more fame by expelling the British from the French port of Toolong by several more Whiffs of Crapshot.

However, Napoleon soon got fed up with being only a Console, & so thought he would have a go at being an Emperor instead. However he soon realised that to be an Emperor it is best to have an Empire also, & this caused the Napoleonic wars as no-one else, especially foreigners, wanted to be any part of his Empire. Thus he knew he would just have to do some conquering, & so he decided to start with Eyegpt, because it was **Strategic**, & anyway, being a Coarsican, he liked the sun & wanted to visit the Pyramids. Not only that, he knew that if he conquered Eyegpt he could cut off the British from India by blocking the Sewage Canal, & then maybe even take India too. He had evidently been reading too much about Alexander the Great!

Bornapart soon set sail with a brand new army & naturally plenty of Crapshot. He also took Bucksheesh to keep the locals happy, & landed near the Pyramids. Here he fought one big battle with the Eyegptian army, which were all Marmadukes. The battle was fought in the shade of the Pyramids as it was an extremely hot day, & naturally Napoleon won, & thus Eyegpt became French, for a time anyway.

Soon dozens of French scientists & archyologists got busy looking for gold & examining & measuring the Pyramids, the Spinks, the Hobbelisks & even Cleopatra's needle! They also dug up all the Faeroes & Faeroesses ect. who were now called "Mummies", but no-one knows why. They even shipped one of the Hobbelisks all the way back to Paris where it can still be seen today. One of them then found the mysterious "Rossiter Stone"[19] which cleverly enabled them to read the Ancient Eyegptian hearoglyphs & thus get a lot of useful information, & more importantly a lot more History. The Faroe Tootancomeon would have turned in his Pyramid!

---

[19] The Ancient Eyegptians never wrote on paper, but on stone or Parchedment.

Meanwhile, the English were getting worried as the French were now blocking the important Sewage canal, thus cutting them off from India where they got all their Spices, Curry & Tandoori powder, seriously undermining the thriving Take-away business. Luckily, however, they still had one more Pitt (who was Youngest) as P.M. who decided that drastic action was needed, & sent the Admirable Lord Nelson to sort things out. Nelson did this by sailing to Eyegpt & utterly sinking the entire French fleet without warning at the extremely Memo-rable Battle of Abooker bay in the Nile.

This left the French completely stigmatised as it was a long way back to France on foot, & they had no big ships left! But the perfhideous Napoleon found a small boat & when the English sailors weren't looking (or the French soldiers, come to that!) he craftily sailed back to France, leaving his army with a very long walk home. Knowing what soldiers are, particularly French ones, the air must have turned blue with "Nom de Dews!" & "Sacred Blues!". This was of course typically Napoleonic & Coarsican, & therefore utterly Unfair.

Having lost one whole army (for the time being, at least) Bornapart soon raised a new one. He had been homesick in Eyegypt, so he decided to have his next Empire closer to home for convenience & for easier commuting (& so he did not have to keep saying "Not Tonight" to Josephine). He also invented a series of Marshals, who were better than just plain generals & thus speeded up the victory rate. All these Marshals had to be brave, but Marshal Nay was Braver. They included Marshal Salt, Marshall Marmite, Marshal Oh do not, Marshall Victoria (a transvestite), Marshall Messana, Marshall Juno, Marshall Bessyairs & Marshall MacDonald (a stray Scotchman). Napoleon also ordered all his soldiers to carry a Marshal's Batten in their napsacks, in case he wanted to make any quick promotions on the battlefield.

Finally, to raise money for his new Empire, Bornapart sold the State of Lousyanna & New Olleans to Jefferson Davis, (see under "The American War of Dependents") who was now President, & said that it was "Manifest Chastity" & part of the "Marilyn Monroe Doctrine"[20] anyway.

Thus prepared, Napoleon next invaded Europe in all directions, much to the consecration of The Austrian Emperors, who were Hapsbugs, the Kings of Prussia (who were Unpronounceable being Kysers, & all called "Bill"), The Kings of Bovaria (who were all mad anyway). The Kings of Spain (who were leftover Bourbons after Louis XVI had been Gilletined), The Sar of Russia (who was an Absolute Ruler), The Kings of Maples (in Italy, also leftover Bonbons), The Dutch, the Deutsch, & last but not least, the P.M. of England, Pitt the Youngest.

The French first invaded Italy, not to fight the Italians, but the Austrians, who inexplicably happened to be there all the time. Bornapart showed great bravery by leading his men across a racketty bridge in a hail of Austrian balls (Cannon & Musket that is) & made his son King of Rome, just to spite the Popes, who had refused to crown him Le Empereur. Then all the other countries got invaded - Austria, Prussia, the Neverlands, Spain, ect., & N. rounded this all off by defeating **ALL** their Armies together at the great battle of Osterlitz!

Meanwhile, the Youngest Pitt, who had by now been renamed Lord Cheatem, devised a clever new way of fighting

---

[20] Which stated that the continent of America utterly belonged to the U.S.A., & no-one else could own any part of it, especially not the English, French or Red Indians.

Napoleonic wars so that English soldiers didn't actually have to fight. This was by a system of Colitions, which meant that all battles on land must be fought by Austrians, Russians, Prussians, Dutch, Spanish, ect., just so long as the Admirable Lord Nelson did all the sea battles for them, & sunk all of Napoleon's fleets, which he did, of course, having already had a lot of practice at it! But unfortunately, Pitt's Colition system in the end didn't work, because (as we have seen) Napoleon defeated all other armies together at Osterlitz, & having thus conquered all other countries, except England, naturally, Bornapart made peace with them all, provided they accepted him as Le Empereur.

Seeing that none of his Colitions had survived, the unfortunate Cheatem (i.e. Pitt Jnr.) rolled up the map, turned the lights out all over Europe & died. This was a disaster for England as it had now completely run out of all kinds of Pitts, whether they were Old, Middle-aged, Young, Younger or Youngest! Thus the country had to roll into a Pitt Stop.

THE NAPOLEONIC INVASION OF ENGLAND (WHICH ACTUALLY DIDN'T HAPPEN)

As he had conquered everything else, Napoleon, not wanting his army to get bored, decided that he must invade England itself! This was the standard procedure of **All** Saber-prattling Dictators[21] who always wanted to (1) Invade England & (2) When they failed to do this to (3) Invade Russia, which was, according to Field Marshal Monty, breaking the 1st Rule

---

[21] E.g. Julia Caesar, Hingist & Horse, Harold Hard Rider, William the Conquistador, the Spanish Ramada, Louis XIV (The Roi Sunburned), William the Orange, Himself of course, the Kyser Bill, Hilter the German Furrier, Muscleeny (who invented Fashism in Italy but lost all his battles), Sadem Hearseain, & Oscar Bin Laydem, ect.

of War which stated "Never invade Russia!", as it will be a flop & anyway was against the Geneva Convention & the U.N.!

Sadly for Bornapart, when he gathered his legions across the Chunnel to invade "Perfhideous Albyon", he soon discovered that there was a distinct shortage of ships, because the Admirable Lord Nelson had sunk the lot! He had even also sunk the entire Danish Navy, (for good measure & to keep his hand in) so that they could not get requisitioned by N. This was the Memorable Battle of Copunhagun, when the Admirable Nelson put his telescope up to his blind eye & memorably declared, "I see no ships!" Actually, of course, he was quite right because by the time he had changed over to the good eye & looked again, all the Danish ships had sunk out of sight below the surface anyway!

So, all this left the French soldiers & poilus (so-called because they were always extremely hairy) high & dry, twiddling their thumbs, smoking their pipes & playing cards on cliffs of Callay, as Nelson had **even** sunk all the Ro-Ro ferries. But this could not go on, as they were getting bored, & were much more used to having Victories. Luckily, however, some bright spark remembered that they, the French, had been the 1st to invent Balloons which meant that they could all cross the Chunnel by air! So Napoleon collected all the balloons in France, & imported a lot of for-eign[22] politicians to provide the Hot Air needed to inflate them. The foreign politicians soon got to work under the balloons, making windy speeches to inflate them. But sadly, whenever the balloons got fully inflated, the wind changed & blew in the wrong direction, & so, as the French did not want to go to Russia (not **yet** anyway!), & **could not** go to England, they

---

[22] There were no local politicians as they had all been abolished by the Gilletine in the French Revelation - see under "French Revulsion".

decided to go & have another war against someone they **knew** they could beat, & it may as well be Austria again! After all, the Austrians were always willing to turn up for a new war & get beaten again.

THE INVASION OF SPAIN

Having duffed up the Austrians, Bornapart thought it would be a nice idea to invade Spain, as he hadn't done that yet. The advantages of this were: (1) Spain was joined up to France by land called the Pyroknees, so his soldiers could invade it easily **without getting their feet wet.** (2) The King of Spain was a leftover Borbon, & Napoleon had decreed that as the Borbon Kings had been well & truly Abolished in France, they must also be abolished everywhere else too! (3) & anyway, he had a brother who wanted a go at being a King, so that might keep **him** quiet!

At first the French did well & easily beat the Regular Spanish Army (though "Regular" must be taken as a very loose term when applied to **any** Spanish Army). The French entered the Capital Mardrid, but then the trouble started because the Spanish did not want a French king, because after all the French didn't have a French king did they? So on Doss de Mao the crowd rose up & massacred the Marmaduke calvary, which had enlisted with France after the battle of the Pyramids in Eyegpt. The Frogs replied to this by massacring the Mardrid crowd with firing squads. Then the war **really** got under way!

The Spanish invented Goryilla warfare as they had run out of "Regular" Armies, & it was a completely new invention. The Goryillas had no uniform & were disguised as regular Spanish pheasants, & were so in clear breeches of the Geneva Convention. Their methods were also unfair to the French soldiers as they invariably let them pass by, & then attacked them from behind their backs. The French had always had their battles from in front, & so had no experience of fighting backwards & so could not cope with the pesky Goryillas. Moreover, attacking from the rear, the Goryillas were invariably atrocious & unexpectedly cut off the arms & legs of the French soldiers when their backs were turned & they weren't looking in the right direction. This was proven by the pictures of the memorable & gruesome Goryilla painter, Gorya, which showed many Gory scenes.

Napoleon now regretted having invaded Spain as it was costing him an arm & a leg (& many of his soldiers both arms & both legs!).

Meanwhile, the English, seeing that the French were finally losing a war, decided to send the Memorable[23] Duke of Wellington to help the atrocious Goryillas. Naturally, being both English & Memorable, Wellington won all his battles & gave the French plenty of Welly. Soon the French in Spain were utterly abolished.

THE ADMIRABLE LORD NELSON

All this time, while the French were becoming armless (& legless) in Spain, Lord Nelson was still sinking French fleets as fast as he could go. Unfortunately, being so brave, he lost a leg, an arm & an eye in these battles, but that didn't stop him! Luckily the French were running out of ships, so Nelson decided to sink their very last fleet & thereby utterly Abolish the French Navy forever. This all happened at Trafalgar, nr. Spain. So he gave the famous message to his men: "England expects every man to get his booty" & then took the French by surprise & sank them all, thereby utterly abolishing them.

---

[23] Memorable because he first invented Boots.

For good measure, & because his blood was up, he also sank the entire Spanish fleet, as it had been foolish enough to be in the vicinity at the time!

Unfortunately this was the Admirable's last battle because he was unfairly shot in the rear Quarto deck by a dastardly Frog snooper up a mast, & as everyone knows the rear Quarto deck is a fatal area. Nelson was carried below, dying, into the bowels of the ship, but it did no good as he was still dying when he got there. He only managed to say to the notoriously transvestite skipper, Hardy, "Kiss me, Hardy", so, as all Great Heroes do, he died with a joke on his lips, although it was rather an iffy joke.

Luckily, although England had ran out of Admirables for the time being, it didn't matter as the French had now completely run out of fleets & ships, in the nick of time. Indeed Nelson had abolished all other Navies, including the Spanish & Danish ones, so the English had no more Navies to fight **at all**, & so their own Navy became **Royal**. The Nation was so grateful to Nelson that they built Trafalgar Square to prove it, which can still be seen & demonstrated in to this day, which is A Very Good Thing.

By this time Napoleon had gotten browned off with the expensive hobby of building new fleets which the English immediately sank, & gave up & abolished his own Navy to save face. So from then on he ordered that all Napoleonic wars had to be fought exclusively on dry land.

THE GRANDEST ARMY & NAPOLEON'S INVASION OF RUSSIA

Like all the other saber-rattling Dictators of Europe, Bornapart just couldn't resist the temptation to invade Russia, thus breaking the Geneva Convention & Field Marshal Monty's 1st Rule of War. This was an utterly foolish decision because:-

1. Russia was very, very big!

2. Russia was very, very, very cold, & the French Army had completely **no Thermal Underwear**!

3. Russia had lousy roads as MacAdam had not yet invented TarMacAdam (Tarmac for short).

4. Russia had many rivers, but very few bridges, & these racketty.

5. Russia had an endless supply of pheasants which were called Muziks, & could be used as cannon fonder.

6. Russia had ferocious calvary called Coffsacks who would kill anyone to order, even their own people!

7. The Sar of Russia was absolutely Absolute.

8. The Russians invariably used a Parched Earth policy, no matter what country they were in, even their own! This meant they destroyed utterly everything the Enemy could use.

9. Russia was uncivilised & Fewdal, & thus still had Surfers & Villains (& the Surfer trade).

Nevertheless, Napoleon grandly renamed his Army "The Grandest Army" & marched for Mosscow. The Russians only fought 1 big battle to stop him, as they had other cunning plans. This was the Battle of Borrowdinner & is well-depicted in the memorable book "War & Peace" by Leon Trotskoy (aka Leo Tollboy). The French then entered Mosscow in short-lived Triumph, & Napoleon pitched his tent in the Kriminalin.

But the Triumph didn't last. All the triumphal French soldiers got drunk on looted Avian water which turned out to actually be Vodker, & as they were all heavy smokers, Mosscow was soon in flames. Napoleon though blamed the Russian

Parched Earth policy & shot all the Muziks he could find, & there weren't many. This did no good however because by this time the city had been utterly elevated & erazed to the ground. Not only this, but the fire also erazed all the Supermarkets & ordinary unsuper Markets, Fast Food inlets, Curry shops, Take-Aways, Bistos & Brassiers, so there wasn't a square meal to be had in the place, not even for one French solider! Worse still, there were no pubs left either & so no Bier or Vin. Even the Vodker was all gone as it was highly inflamed. Enraged, Bornapart swiftly ordered a Smoking Ban in all Public Places, but as there were no Public Places left anyway, it did utterly no good!

Napoleon had to order the Memorable Retreat from Mosscow as it was also getting colder & colder. The journey back to France was a terrible one for the Grandest Arméé as the terrible Coffsack calvary kept harassing it in its rears & so, once again, the French had to fight **backwards** (like in Spain against the Goryillas - see earlier), & most of them were only used to fighting **frontwards**! Marshal Nay, who was the bravest of most, defended the rears in the Vanguard, but with the horrible Coffsacks attacking all the time, the Grandest Arméé became less & less grand, until it was only Grander & then just grand with a small "g", ect. To make matters worse there was gridlock at the racketty Berrysinner bridge, so not too many got across. By the time it got back to France the army was not so much grand as ground (down to nothing).

This then was the downfall of Napoleon as he had used up all his grand or not-so-grand Arméés by now, & so the Sar, Wellington & Metternick, the Australian Chancellus egg-siled him to be Emperor of Elbow, a small island somewhere in Italy. The Borbon Kings were restored & renovated & the poor French had to put up with yet another Louis, their XVIIIth! (Louis XVII seems to have got lost in the backwash somewhere.) Louis XVIII was fat & ugly (a Borbon tradition) like all the other Louis's from I thru XVII, but like Charles II he wanted to die with his boots off, so he let them keep their Tricorner flag. (The Borbon flag had been white with white lily-livers on it.) However, unwisely he refused to let his subjects take any more Liberties, nor Eggalities & Friternities. He decreed that only visiting Americans could continue to take Liberties, which of course they did as that was their inviolate & invariable custom.

THE 100 DAYS

Napoleon Bornapart soon got browned off with being Emperor of Elbow. For one thing there was not room enough on the Italian island for his troops to manhoover properly. The natives spoke a strange language & ate only spaghetty, pissa or Gorgonzola cheese, & drank a wine called Keyanti, which came in straw covered bottles & had a bouquet, taste & consistency which closely approximated to that of paraffin. Moreover, on the island there were no Liberties to take, let alone Eggalities & Friternities! So, in the circs, Napoleon decided to thin out & do a runner which he had already shown he was good at, as he had successfully run away from Eyegpt, Spain & Russia. His objective was to go back to France, become Empereur again & grant himself Political Asylum!

Meanwhile Marshal Nay, who was good at changing sides (he preferred to be on the side that was winning) had be-come C-in-C of the Borbon army. When he heard of Napoleon's landing he promised Louis XVIII that he would bring him back to Paris in an iron box. But when he met with Napoleon his (Nay's) Borbon troops, most of whom were ex-Napoleon-ics, refused to fire on Le Empereur, & changed sides without even changing their uniforms. To save the situation Nay said, "Nay, je ne peut pas desert mon Empereur" & also changed sides as he saw Napoleon as a likely winner. Together they marched on Paris, leaving the said metal box to rust by the roadside.

Meanwhile, in Paris, seeing that his army had been converted back to Napoleonics, the old, fat & ugly XVIIIth Louis wisely decided that it was time to thin out, so he too did a runner & made himself as scarce as he could in the circum-stances. Napoleon re-entered Paris in Triomphe, & built the Arch de Triomphe (near the Chumps Eeleasy) to prove it (which can still be seen today).

A shudder went through all the other European countries, as they did not want to be again reconquered, reconstituted & renovated by the French at the point of the bayonnet. So the English sent for the memorable Duke of Wellington who had already given the French a fair bit of Welly in Spain.

THE DUKE OF WELLINGTON & WATERLOO

The memorable Duke of Wellington was popular with his troops who called him "The Iron Juke" & some less compli-mentary things to Boot (usually connected with his over-large nosal organ). He fondly called his soldiers "the slum of the Earth", but they took this as a complement as they were mostly ex-soccer hooligans from Man. U & Liverpool, & Morale rose accordingly.

The British were soon in Belgium (The Lowest of the Low countries) & so they had a Ball in Brussels, which was just as well as it was the last Ball many of them did have, actually.

The next morning they marched out to battle, hungover but still with their Morale high.

The Iron Juke very strategically decided not to manhoover, as manhoovering anywhere near Napoleon was an iffy business, so he seized the Morale high ground on a hill called Waterloo & stayed put. He then showed his ingenius by ingenuously arranging his troops in new formations, thin red lines, thin red squares & thin red other mathematical figures, ect. When the French saw the thin red lines & squares they were utterly baffled & did not know what to make of it at all! So Marshal Nay was sent up Waterloo hill with all the French calvary, & although he charged more than 20 times he still could not work out the meaning of the thin red lines, squares, parallelograms, ect. So then the French infantry went forward, but Wellington booted them down again with copious Whiffs of Crapshot.

While all this was happening the Prussians under the memorable Marshal Blooper[24] were beginning to move in on the French flanks & rears unnoticed by Napoleon who was mesmorised by the thin red squares, ect.

Meanwhile, in desperation Bornapart now ordered the Old Guard up the hill. The Old Guard were all big men with utterly ferocious moustaches & tall hats made of sheepskin. This was an unpresidented move as usually the Old Guard were kept out of all battles because it might spoil their nice uniforms.

As the Old Guard advanced up the hill, The Juke gave the famous order: "Up Guards & Bat 'em!" (as it is well known that

---

[24] Marshal Blooper later visited London & was given a view of the city. The story goes that he said (in German), "What a place to plunder," when in fact he said, "What a ruddy colossal blunder," as he was watching Eastenders at the time!

the Battle of Waterloo was won on the Playing Fields of Eden, actually). The whole British line moved forward chanting, "'Ere we go, 'Ere we go, 'Ere we go / 'Ere we go, 'Ere we go, 'Ere we go-oo," ect. (just as the Ancient Brits had done when they saw Julia Caesar – see under "The Ancient Brits") & with the Scotch pipers to the four. The Old Guard had never before heard the Scotch pipes, & they thought it was the end of the World so they scarpered Toot sweet in all directions at once. The rest of the French army was already fleeing, & the lights were going out all over Bornapart.

Wellington had showed great courage, riding around the battle-field with balls flying all around him without flinching. But his companion. Lord Oxbridge lost a leg to a difficult ball. He survived though & had a handsome replacement made in carved oak, of which he was justly proud.

Thus Napoleon had felt the weight of the Wellington boot, so he retired to Mount St. Helena & utterly ceased to be Historically memorable. Everyone breathed a sigh of relief, even the French.

THE CONGRESS OF VIENNA

After Waterloo a big Congress was held in Vienna to round off the Napoleonic Wars once & for all & finally. This was the idea of the Austrian Chancelus Maeterlink. All the Royals & Top Statesmen of Europe met & had Congress there. They also agreed on a new set of Rules, which were called "The Maeterlink System" & said that:-

1. Napoleon was utterly abolished forever, & there were to be absolutely no new Napoleons whatever, of any shape, size or description!

2.   Revolutions were illegal & therefore utterly banned in all Public places.

3.   There was to be "Divide & Rule" & all ordinary people must be Divided up & Ruled (which must have been very uncomfortable).

4.   The Gilletine was completely abolished, & from then on everyone must be shot or hanged, or both.

5.   Liberals (people who wanted Constitutionals) were utterly banned.

6.   Italy was to be ruled by Austrians, the Pope & the Bonbon Kings of Maples only, because the Ities had been too friendly to Bornapart.

7.   Poland must once again be partitioned (cut up) & the partitions shared out between Russia, Prussia & Austria, because Napoleon had had a Polish mistress (over & above Josephine, his Empress).

This system worked well, & a great time was had by all (that is all the Royals & Top Statesmen, but nobody else). That is until 1848, the "Year of Revolutions" when all countries had Revolutions simultaneously, except England of course, which had persuaded all English Revolutionaries to make a Chart instead (Chartism) - see next chapter.

As for Maeterlink, he had to escape from the revolting Viennese Rabbles by hiding in a laundry basket, in which he got laundered & somehow lost in the backwash!

Historical Aptitude & Intelligence Test

Test Paper 7: The Industrial Revelation & Napoleonic Wars
(1 hour 30 mins)

1. Why was the invention of the Working class so important?

2. Discuss the importance of the following in Science & the Industrial Revelation: (a) Apples (b) All Chemists (c) Dark Satanic Mills (d) Mess - Production (e) Steam Rockets.

3. Was Islambard Kingdom Brunel a genius or a megalomaniac? Or both!

4. What was the main cause of Napoleon? Was he a Good Thing?

5. What was the hysterical importance of: (a) A Whiff of Crapshot (b) The Rossiter Stone (c) The Sewage Canal (d) Manifest Chastity (e) The Battle of Osterlitz?

6. Why was Napoleon's invasion of England a total failure?

7. What was the importance of the Admirable Lord Nelson? What did he mean when at Trafalgar he gave the order: "England expects every man to get his Booty"?

8. Describe the Spanish use of Goryilla Warfare.

9. Why did Nelson say, "Kiss me, Hardy," to Captain Hardy?

10. Why did Navies in Europe go out of fashion in the time of Lord Nelson?

11. In the context of Bornapart's invasion of Russia, what was the importance of: (a) Muziks (b) Coffsacks (c) Vodker (inflamed) (d) A smoking ban in Public places.

12. Why did Napoleon get fed up with being Emperor of the island of Elbow?

13. At the Battle of Waterloo what was the importance of the following: (a) Thin red lines (b) Thin red Squares (c) Prussian Marshal Blooper (d) "Up Guards and Bat 'em!" (e) The Playing fields of Eden (f) Marshal Nay (g) Scotch pipes.

14. Give a profile of the Iron Juke.

15. What did the Chancellus of Austria, Maeterlink, Abolish at the Congress of Vienna? Why was Poland Abolished?

16. How did Maeterlink get lost in the backwash?

THE END!

H.A.I.T. Test Paper 7:
Model Answer Specimen

1. The invention of the Working class during the Industrial Revelation was hysterically important because it meant that England became the Sweatshop of the World, & deported all its new products to the Empire, ect. It also allowed everyone who **wasn't** Working class to get very rich, & made the poor utterly suffer for it!

2. (a) Apples were important to Sir Isaac Norton because he noticed that they **never fell upwards**, & so Gravity was invented, & even made into a **Law**.

(b) There was a notable outbreak of Alchemists who were All Chemists, & not just Apostrophes who only made drugs, during the 18th century. These All Chemists notably made Bass metal into gold by a secret formula.

(c) Dark Satanic Mills were the invention of the poet William Bleak, & this resulted in the "Bleak country" up North, & Jerusalem in England's Green & Pleasant land, not to mention Burning Arrows of Desire. But unluckily this also sometimes caused "Trouble at Mill" because rioting Weevils called Lyddites often broke the machines, because they were revolting at the time.

(d) Mess-Production was a result of the Industrial Revulsion, but it made Bags of Brass & was therefore A Good Thing.

(e) Steam Rockets were invented by Stephenson, who also invented Steam Trains.

3. The Memorable Engineer Islambard Kingdom Brunel built Railways, Tunnels (mainly under the Thames), bridges & utterly enormous Steam Ships. His railways & steam

ships were all "Great" Somethings, e.g. the Great Eastern Railway, & The Great Western ship. Brunel also invented a new way to launch his gargantuan Ships - sideways, which was new at the time. He was thus both an Ingenuous **And** a Megalomanic. He smoked a lot though, even in Public places!

4. Napoleon was hysterically important to the French because all the other French Pollyticians had Gilletined each other during the French Revulsion, & so there were none left. But there was also a Revolting Parris Rabbles (Sank-alots) left over from the Revulsion, so he had to abolish this with a "Whiff of Crapshot", thus totally cancelling the Revulsion & restoring Law & Order.

5. (a) After the successful Abolition of the Revolting Paris mob, Bornapart carried on using Whiffs of Crapshot to abolish the Prussian, Russian, Austrian, Spanish & Dutch armies, so it was a useful tactic to the aspiring Empereur.

(b) The utterly Memorable Rossiter Stone was dug up in Eyegpt by French Archyologists & helped them to transmute the Ancient Eyegptians, who only wrote on stones or parchedment.

(c) The French blocked the Sewage Canal by invading Eyegpt. This held up British Curry supplies from India & Parkeystan, a grievous loss which totally undermined the booming Take-away trade & Curry shops. Even the Admirable Lord Nelson could not unblock it.

(d) "Manifest Chastity" meant that the U.S. could steal utterly all the land in America from the Red Indians & anyone else who was there. It was also called the Marilyn

Monroe Doctrine, & came as a result of the Lousyanna Purchase from the French (New Olleans, ect.).

(e) Napoleon Bornapart beat ALL the other Armies at Osterlitz, & forced Lord Cheatem (the Youngest & last Pitt) to roll up the Map of Europe & switch all the lights out (as his Colitis system had failed).

6. Napoleon failed to invade England because the Admirable Lord Nelson kept sinking his fleets (even in Eyegpt) as fast as they were built. Having no ships to cross the Chunnel, & not wanting Nelson to sink his Armies as well as his Navies, Napoleon decided to use Hot Air Balloons. But in spite of importing Pollyticians from all over Europe, they could not produce enough Hot Air to inflate the Balloons, & anyway there was a chronic shortage of Balloonatics. So the French army had to go back & beat the Austrians again.

7. The Admirable Lord Nelson was hysterically important because he totally abolished the French Navy, time & time again, mainly by sinking it. He had a sense of humour too as whenever the French ships had sunk he would put his telescope up to his blind eye saying, "I see no ships!", get it? His comment at Trafalger that "England expects every man to get his Booty" meant that there was a lot of loot in it for the English Materlots.

8. Goryilla warfare was against the Geneva Convention because the Spanish Goryillas always attacked from the Rears, & the hapless French Army had only been trained to fight **Frontwards**, not **Backwards**. The Goryillas were utterly Atrocious too as they invariably cut the arms & legs off the French soldiers, making them both harmless & legless to Boot. We know all this from the Gory pictures of

the memorable Spanish painter Gorya! Even Napoleon himself also found that the Spanish war was costing him an Arm & a Leg.

9. "Kiss me, Hardy" was the Admirable Lord Nelson's last words at the Battle of Trafalgar - an iffy joke at the expense of the notoriously Transvestite, Captain Hardy!

10. European Navies went out of fashion in Europe because Nelson sank them all, not only the French one, but also the Danish, Dutch & Spanish ones too! No-one thought it was worthwhile building New Navies, especially while **HE** was around.

11. (a) Muziks were the limitless supply of Russian pheasants who could be used as Cannon fodder against Bornapart.

(b) Coffsacks were the ferocious & atrocious Russian calvary who would kill anyone, especially French soldiers from the Rears.

(c) Vodker was the cause of the burning of Mosscow in 1812, because the French soldiers mistook it for Avian water & got so drunk that they set fire to the city. Vodker burned well too because it was highly Inflammatory.

(d) Napoleon was extremely cross at the accidental burning of Mosscow by careless French Buttends, so he banned smoking in all Public places. But this was fertile as there were no Public places left after the Great Fire!

12. Bornapart soon got browned off with the island of Elbow, as there was no room for manhoover for his troops, who were getting too fat on the local Spaghetty & Gorgonzola. Also he wanted to take more Liberties, but **not** Eggality or Friternity.

13. (a) Thin red lines & (b) Thin red squares were the invention of the Juke of Wellington at Waterloo, which kept the French guessing. They suspected that this was a crafty conspiracy by the Perfhideous Albinos.

(c) Marshal Blooper & his Prussian army arrived late for the Battle of Waterloo, but when they **did** arrive they penetrated Napoleon's Flanks & Rears.

(d) Wellington memorably said, "Up Guards and Bat 'em," referring to cricket played on the (e) Playing fields of Eden.

(f) Marshal Nay was very brave, but kept changing sides to be on the Winning one.

(g) Scotch Pipes played a big part at Waterloo because they stampeded & disposed Napoleon's Old Guard all over the place & Utterly.

14. Wellington, the Iron Juke, was gifted with a gigantic nose & was Nosey. He gave the Frogs plenty of Welly in Spain, & then finished them off with a Waterloo.

15. The Congress of Vienna abolished practically everything including Napoleon, Revolutions, Liberals, Liberties, Poland, the Gilletine, Freedom of Speech, ect. This was the Maeterlink system of dividing people up, especially the Polish, then Ruling them!

16. Maeterlink escaped from the Revolting Viennese Rabbles in a laundry basket. Unfortunately he was then accidentally laundered together with all his money, & then got utterly lost in the backwash due to a computer error.

CHAPTER 8
GEORGE IV, WILLIAM IV & THE VICTORIAN ERRAR

THE PRINCE REGNANT

When George III died there was still one George left over, the Prince Regnant who naturally became the IVth. But he was a dissoluted man, very fat & unpopular, as well as being heels over head in Debit & Disgust. He was in love with Mrs. Fitzturbot who was already married, & an R.C. which was illegal. Moreover since she was common, marrying her would be Magnetic. So the P.M. arranged for George to be married to Princess Carolyn of Burnswick instead. But when George saw her he ordered a stiff drink & leave the bottle! Unsurprisingly Carolyn was offended by this, & toured Europe in Pink Tights & with an Italian Latin lover called Biryani, & so she became common too (which may be why the common people liked her). Even so, at the Coronation she was locked out, & beat the door with her brolly. So, with all this scandal & disgrace George died pretty soon, & good riddance everyone said, including even the *Times*.

The next King was William IV as all the Georges had been used up, but he was just a sailor & never quite figured out how to be a King.

ENGLAND AFTER WATERLOO

The Industrial Revulsion continued (see earlier), causing more & more pheasants to move to towns, but this caused more Working class who were not happy about being poor & Sweat-shopped when all the Astrocrats, Lords & Naybobs lived on the Lip of Luxury. This caused many workers to become Radicles who demanded Universal Suffering to make the Astrocrats, Lords & Naybobs suffer as much as them. They also demanded the Frenchsize which meant they wanted the Vote, & were nearly Revolutionaries. This started Rabbles & Revolting, but the Iron Juke stepped in & massacred them with a Whiff of Calvary at Peterloo, another great Victory.

But this did not altogether do the trick as the Radicles continued to be Revolting, especially to the Lyddites & Captain Swing (so-called because the Naybobs said that if they ever caught him he would surely Swing).

Wellington was now P.M. & a Tory, so he tried to stop the Radicles by Catholic Emaciation, but even this did not work, so in the end Parliament had to enact the Great Reform Bill.

THE GREAT REFORM ACT

To quieten everything down, the Middle class which had just been invented, were given the Frenchsize so that they could vote, but not the Working class, naturally, as they must continue suffering & become Carpists. The Act also utterly abolished Rotten Burrows & even Pocket Burrows where only 1 person had the vote & therefore voted for himself, naturally.

Luckily William IV now died & it was decided as everyone was so fed up with Georges & even Williams, that they would make a young girl Queen, as there hadn't been one since Glory Anna. This therefore began the Victorian Errar, which mainly solved the problem. Victoria started her reign young which is why She lasted so long.

THE ROMANTIC ERRAR

Because of the French Revulsion & the Industrial Revelation, there was an outbreak of Romantics, who liked the French Revulsion, but hated the Mess-production of the Industrial Revulsion with all its Unromantic Saturnic Mills, ect. To be a Romantic it was compulsory to also be a Poet, a Painter or a Writer, like Lord Biro, William Wordsmith, Pursey Bish Shelly (& wife Mary), Sir Walter Scotch, John Keets, ect.

The most Romantic of these was the utterly Romantic poet Lord Biro, who wrote a very long poem called Don Juran, & was very popular with the ladies who said he was Mad, Bad & Dangerous to know, but looked like a Geek God. As it happened the Geeks were having a War of Independents at the time, so Lord Biro went to Grease & died extremely Romantically.

This inspired another Romantic Lord called Eggin to go to Grease & rip all the Eggin Marbles off the Parfenon in Athens (a big Ancient Geek temple) for deportation to England, where they would be safe from Vandals. When the Geek customs men asked Lord Eggin what he had in the crates, he said, "It's only Marbles," so they thought he must have lost his & let him through. It wasn't until he was long gone that they discovered that they in fact were the ones who had lost their Marbles. As for the "Marbles", they actually turned out to be beautiful Ancient Geek statues, though most of them had lost vital parts of the body. They have been correctly kept in the British Museum ever since.

Other famous Romantics included the poet William Word-smith who wrote about lonely clouds & hosts of Golden Daffodils, which was also Romantic, but less so. There was also Percy Bish Shelley who also wrote good poetry, while his wife Mary wrote excellent fiction about Frankinstyne, Drackula, Vampires, Werewolves, ect., which were Romantic but weird.

QUEEN VICTORIA

Queen Victoria was young when she became Queen, & said she **would** be good, but would never be amused. She kept her word too.

At about this time England got a new & memorable P.M. called Ken John Peal. He did several more reforms & in-vented Policemen & repealed the Bow street running club. Most notably he repealed[25] the Corn Laws, so that Corns could be deported into England to help the Irish who had run out of Potatoes. This was important since it ended Trade Protectivism.

Meanwhile Roland Hill invented Postage Stamps with a picture of the severed (or severe) Queen's head on them, & they only cost 1p. You could have them in two colours, Red or Black, according to taste. This, of course, gave rise to the Royal Male.

LORD PUMICESTONE

Another notable figure of the time was the utterly memorable Lord Pumicestone ("Pum" for short), who became first an M.P,

---

[25] Peal never abolished things, he always Repealed them!

then an F.M., & finally a P.M. (but not necessarily in that order). He didn't like Foreigners, especially if they were Natives, & insisted that they must **Always** be Nice to the British, & when they weren't he always sent a Gunboat & bombarded them until they were. He even sent the Gun-boats as far away as China to abolish the evil Opium trade, but all they could find to bombard there was a load of Chinese Junks & Chinese Junk Food stalls. Pumicestone also promoted the expansion of the Empire, which meant there had to be many colonyalist wars to keep the Army busy.

THE EXPANSION OF THE EMPIRE ON WHICH THE SUN NEVER SAT

Lord Pumicestone believed in this & so there were many colonyal wars, e.g. 2 or 3 Opium Wars, 2 Afghan Wars, 2 Bore Wars, a Zuloo war, a Shanty war, & even an Indian Mutilation, to name but a few. The Empire kept on expanding in all directions. Malaysia became British, & they discovered Rubber, which of course has many vital uses. Sir Stanford Ruffles built Singerpore, & the British even got as far as the exotic island of Bornio where they fought the local Dykes who had long blowpipes & often gave the Redcoats the benefit of the Dart. They also discovered the N.E. Passage or "Up the Khyber", & even took some bits of China. Later Lord Chumpsford had a war with the savage but Noble Zuloos under their King Getawayo (see under "An Unsuccessful Colonyal War") & finally they expelled all the Old Bores from South Africa on the Great Truck.

This kept the British well-supplied with Wars (a normal British policy in any errar) & kept the soldiers out of trouble at home, which was A Good Thing. Whenever they ran out of colonyal wars, they were smart enough to invent things like

The Crimean War to keep the pot boiling (see later). Needless to say, The British **Always Won!**

THE ROYAL WEDDING

Queen Victoria married Prince Albert of Sacks-Coalbag, a mining district of Germany. Albert was the best King England never had, but as he wasn't as Royal as Queen Victoria, he could not be a real King but had to be Prince Consulate instead. To keep him busy, the Queen started him on some building projects like the Museum of National Science, The National Science Museum, the Albert Hall, the Albert Manorial, Ballmoral Castle &, of course, the well-known Albert square. This was a Good Thing as it kept him from interfering with her Red missmatch boxes. Marrying Albert meant that the Queen could no longer be a Hunnoverian, & had to be a Sack-Coalbag instead. Much later the Royal family turned into Winsors, as Sack-Coalbags were not thought to be Patriotic at the time (just as Lord Battenbug changed into Montbatten).

THE CRIMEAN WAR

Owing to a temporary shortage of Colonyal wars, the British now decided to have a war in Russia. This was because the Russians had started bullying the nice Otterman Turks to get the Darningneedles which would give them access to the Mediterranean, which would mean the British would have to sink yet another Navy. So to the Turkish Delight, England decided to siege Servastapole (though it is not clear why).

The Crimean war was so-called as it was against the proper Rules & a Crime against the Geneva Convention. Even so, the English generals were notably ALL Lords. The C-in-C was Lord Ragman, & Lord Look-on & Lord Cardigan were i/c the

Calvary. There were several battles in this war, all of which naturally the British won, but the most Memorable & Romantic of these was the Battle of Ballyclava because it had:- (1) A charge of the Heavy Brigade (2) A charge of the Light Brigade & (3) A thin red line. (But not necessarily in that order.)

THE CHARGE OF THE LITE BRIGADE

This was such an Utterly Memorable event that the Celebrity Poet Lorryeat, Alfred Laud Tinnyson wrote a special Poem about it. It happened like this: first the Heavy Brigade charged under Lord Look-on. But the Light Brigade under Lord Cardigan were jealous of this & were utterly determined to charge **Something** no matter what it was! So Lord Cardigan, who had absolutely **No** sense of direction whatever charged in exactly the **Wrong** direction. But the crafty Russians had put Guns to the left of him, Guns to the right of him, Guns in front of him, & even Guns behind him, so whichever way he charged the Light Brigade was getting utterly shot up. Amazingly, Lord Cardigan survived, but the Light Brigade did not.

Meanwhile the thin red line was doing its bit by shooting any Russian calvary left over from the battle. Thus the British won, because the Charge was Utterly Glorious, & thus a Very Good Thing.

After the battle, the British did not know quite what to do with all the Russian guns captured by the Light Brigade, so they spent the rest of the war melting them down & making them into new Medals called Victoria Crosses.

As for Lord Cardigan, he had had enough of battles, so he spent the rest of the war on his yacht inventing & knitting nice woolly Cardigans for any of his men left over from the Charge. Finally Servastapole luckily fell & thus the war ended.

THE INDIAN MUTILATION

The India Company (in India), having run out of British soldiers owing to the Black Hole of Calcutter (a particularly
unpleasant Night Club), & of course the Crimean War, began
to employ Indian soldiers called Seapoys instead. This seemed
satisfactory until the Seapoys were issued with a new rifle.
Their officers told them that they must bite the bullet before
firing it, but the Seapoys didn't like the taste of the bullets, &
anyway it was against their Religions to bite bullets whatsoever, so they refused. They also sent secret messages all around
India disguised in piles of Chip Butties (or Chop Patties).

The Seapoys then Mutilated against their officers, led by a
Seapoy called Pandy (1st name Andy) & became Rabbles,
taking the capital Deli, & be seiging Cornpore & No Lucknow
& causing utterly frightful Atrocities & Mutilations. Luckily
the British still had the Highland (Scotch) division which
immediately formed thin red lines & squares & attacked the
Mutilations who got unutterably mutilated & deafened to
boot by the Snarl of the Pipes. Thus the Indian Rabbles were
quickly reduced to Rubbles. Deli & No Lucknow were very
relieved to see the Scotch soldiers. As for the Mutilaters, many
of them were shot from cannon, which saved the time &
trouble of burying them as they were now for the birds.

To keep the leftover Indians, Q. Victoria graciously resigned
from being just a Queen & became an Empress instead.

GLADSTERN & DIZZRAELI

At about this time it was decided that one P.M. was not
enough to cope with all the new Factory Acts, Mines Acts,
Irish church disembowellment Acts, Harm Rule Acts, Frenchsize & Sufferage Acts that were occurring all over the place.

So it was decided to have 2 P.M.s for the rest of the Century who would take turns at being P.M. while the other took a holiday. The first two chosen were Gladstern & Dizzraeli:-

1. Gladstern was more stern than Glad, & soon got the nickname GOM ("Grumpy Old Man"). Even the Queen did not like him because he kept addressing her at Public meetings in a very loud voice. He also had some very strange Hobbies like chopping down trees & lifting up Fallen Women in Eastenders.

2. Gladstern didn't like wars & favoured "Piece, Entrenchment & Reform". But the English loved their Colonyal Wars, & so GOM got very unpopular when he refused to relieve General Gordon who was being be sieged in Kartomb by fantastic Mardies, Willing Durvishes & Fuzzy-Wuzzies (see later).

3. But he made up for this by Disembowelling the Irish churches, passing Harm Rule & founding Bored Schools which made children give up mining & spinning in factories. Whether the Bored School children were pleased about this is, however, utterly doubtful.

4. Dizzyraeli (or "Dizzy") was much more urban & well-mannered than Gladstern, & so the Queen liked him much better, especially as he had nicer hobbies, writing Romantic novels & poetry. He was also a much greater International statesman than GOM, & spent much time solving Balcan problems & Burgarian massacres in Congresses in Berlin, ect.

GENERAL GORDON[26] IN KARTOMB

At this time the natives were getting restless in the Soodan. Having run out of English armies, we sent an Eyegyptian one instead under Hicks Basher. But the fantastical Mardies, Willing Durvishes & Fuzzy-Wuzzies[27] unutterably abolished & repealed Hicks Basher & his army altogether. This left General Gordon being be sieged in Kartomb on his own, & unfortunately when Kartomb fell, he too was abolished.

The British public blamed GOM for all this, although in actual fact he was nowhere near Soodan whatsoever at the time. Luckily, in the nick of time, General Lord Kitchen was sent out, & cleared up the whole thing by winning the last battle at Kartomb & putting the Mardi out to Grass.

AN UNSUCCESSFUL COLONYAL WAR

To keep the Colonyalist wars on the boil, Lord Chumpsford decided to stir up a tribe of fierce black Worriers in South Africa called Zuloos, under their King, Getawayo. These Zuloos didn't have armies but Impeys, but there were no Wimps in the Impeys. All this proved to be unwise because the Zuloos did not fight in thin red lines or even thin red squares, which was what the British were used to. Instead, they fought with Bulls horns, Assyguys (a type of spear) & Nob Curries (a kind of club). This took Lord Chumpsford & his army totally by surprise at the battle of Iceandwaner & they were absolutely abolished & An-Nihil-ated unutter-

---

[26] One of the famous & utterly memorable Gay Gordons.

[27] The Fuzzy-Wuzzies were fierce dessert warriors who, according to the writer Rudeyard Kipping, could actually break thin red British squares & even thin red lines. They were so-called because they all had fabulous Afro hairstyles.

ably, which was definitely Not a Good Thing. However, a few soldiers held out at O'Rourke's drift, thus proving that British was still best. Consequentially, the British won in the end, locked up Getawayo & utterly abolished all Bull's Horns, Assyguys & Nob Curries.

THE BORE WAR

The Bores were South African farmers, also called Africaners because they were always caning Africans. They did not like to be ruled by the British, so they had to be driven out in the Great Truck. These Boretruckers then formed their own Boring Republics further North (but still in Africa), but after the unsuccessful Zuloo war, the British yerned for a successful Colonyal war. So, after gold was discovered in the Boring Republic of Transvall, a load of British Gold-diggers moved in to dig it. This caused friction between Cecil Roads, a famous British Gold-digger who founded Roadesia, & the Boring President Kruder of the Transvall, & thus gave the British a good excuse for war.

At first the war did not go very well as the Bore Commandos were awfully good shots with their Schnauzer rifles, & some British soldiers unexpectedly found that they were dead before they had even **seen** a Bore, which, when all is said & done, was a real Bore. Also these upstartling Bore Truckers did not fight at all fair as they wore no proper uniforms & shot from behind rocks & trees, ect., instead of fighting correctly in thin red lines & thin red squares. They also used Long Johns to fire big shells into Mafficking, which was an utterly uncouth & atrocious thing to do. They even fired these Long Johns at Lady Smith too, which lacked shivalry.

However, Queen Victoria now told the British that they absolutely **must** win the war as the Bores were only farmers whatever happened, so she sent Winston Churchill out in an armoured train. But the dastardly Bores defiled the armoured train & locked Winston up. But Winston escaped back down the railway line, & after that things began to improve.

The Queen then sent 2 new Generals, Bob & Kitchen, & Rudeyard Kipping wrote a song about Boots moving up & down again, & this encouraged the soldiers no end. They locked up all the Boring women & children in Consecration camps, & so the British won after all when the Bore General Smut surrendered. This gave great Relief to Mafficking, & gave rise to Baydon Paul's Boy Scouts, not forgetting Mrs. Baydon Paul's Girl Guys. All this was, naturally, A Very Good Thing!

THE END OF HISTORY

Queen Victoria died correctly in 1900 & this marks the end of History because after this date everything became MODERN & therefore NOT HISTORY because:-

1. Planes were invented by the Write brothers at Kitty-wake & this caused cheap package holidays.

2. Cars were invented by Rolls, Royce, Ben Daimler & their girlfriend Mercedes. This caused modern Spaghetti junctions, Gridlock, Road Rage & Parking tickets.

3. Electricity was invented which meant that the lights could go out all over Europe.

4. Macaroni invented Wireless Radio & sent it across the Atlantic.

5. Alexander Gayman Bell invented Telephones, which caused telephone bills.

6. Kayser Bill invented Barbed wire & Machine guns, & also the War To End All Wars, which didn't. But it did lead to the utter abolition of all Emperors, Kings, Sars in Europe, & even Kayser Bill himself. This led inevitably to an outbreak of Presidents & Republics.

7. Women Suffering Jets got the vote by chaining themselves to lamp posts, race horses, ect. This caused shorter skirts & licensing behaviour like the Charleston.

8. John Yogi Bear invented Television.

9. The Labour party was invented by socialising Working classes, who were Generally Struck by their 1st P.M. Keer Harding.

10. Communism was invented by Carl Marks, Lennon, Stalion & Troksy, & later even spread as far as China by Meow Ze Tongue.

11. On sweet bathrooms came in with modern plumming.

12. Hitler marched on Poland, but got beaten in the end by Winston Churchill who fought him on the beaches (& the Spitfire).

13. Newclear War was invented by America & tested out on Nagger Sarky.

14. America bombed Vetnam & made it into an unutterable Quagmeyer.

15. Nurds invented the Internut & E-Males.

16. Ect., ect.

So, for the above reasons, as everything after 1900 was Modern, History ended too.

***

N.B. This is not quite THE END, as Test Paper No. 8 is overleaf - ALL candidates should attempt ALL questions!

Historical Aptitude & Intelligence Test
Test Paper 8: The Victorian Errar
(1 hour 30 mins)

1. Why did Princess Carolyn tour Europe in pink tights with a Latin lover called Biryani?

2. Why did the Radicle Working class demand Universal Suffering (or the Frenchsize)?

3. Why were Rotten Burrows & Pocket Burrows **wrong**?

4. Explain the importance of: (a) Lord Biro (b) The Eggin Marbles (c) P.M. Ken John Peal (c) The Bow street Running club (d) The Royal Male.

5. Why did the Romantics dislike the Industrial Revulsion, Mess-Production & Dark Saturnic Mills?

6. Explain Lord Pumicestones Foreign Policy.

7. Why was Prince Albert of Sacks-Coalbag, the Prince Consulate, the best King England never had?

8. Explain the significance of: (a) The Charge of the Light Brigade (b) Lord Look-on (c) The thin red line (d) The Black Hole of Calcutter (e) Chip Butties (or Chop Patties) in India.

9. What caused the Indian Mutilation?

10. Why was the famous writer Rudeyard Kipping concerned about things like: (a) Fuzzy-Wuzzies (b) Boots (c) Jungle Books.

11. With reference to the Zuloo war explain: (a) Bull Horns (b) Assyguys (c) Nob Curries (d) O'Rourke's Drift.

12. Who were the Bore Truckers & why?

13. Explain the importance of the following during the Bore War: (a) Schnauzer rifles (b) Long Johns (c) Lady Smith (d) Consecration camps (e) Girl Guys.

14. Write short notes on: (a) John Yogi Bear (b) Gridlock (c) Alexander Gayman Bell (d) Nurds (e) On Sweet bathrooms (f) The Suffering Jets.

THE END!

***

And the Best of Luck.

ACKNOWLEDGEMENTS

Thanks to Anne-Marie McManus for all her help and assistance with editing and publishing this book. Thanks to Kim and Sinclair Macleod, and Rachel Hessin at Indie Authors World for their care and attention in turning this type-written manuscript into a book Stuart would be proud of.

ABOUT THE AUTHOR

Stuart Campbell MacPherson (1943-2018) was born in Maidstone, Kent. He had a daughter and a son, and later settled in Fort William. He had an M.A., and graduated from Jesus College, Oxford in 1965 with a major in History. As a secondary/tertiary teacher, Stuart worked in the UK, Spain, the Bahamas, Singapore, Brunei (Borneo), Australia and Saudi Arabia.

After many years of research, Stuart wrote three books before he had a stroke. This book represents one part of his legacy.

Milton Keynes UK
Ingram Content Group UK Ltd.
UKHW041926131023
430523UK00004B/63

9 781916 146242